500
ALPHABETS
IN CROSS STITCH

500
ALPHABETS
IN CROSS STITCH

J U L I E   H A S L E R

Text by
VALERIE JANITCH

David & Charles

Above: This Framecraft box makes an ideal travel sewing kit. With a fitting message stitched onto its 18-count pincushion lid using two strands, it can contain all you will need for quick repairs. The alphabet is on Chart 94.

Page 2: The Well-Dressed Home

Comfort and style are combined in these attractive accessories for the home. A 14-count ruffled hoop carries a welcome message emphasised by strands of cotton (floss) picking out the strong colours in the floral frill and using the alphabet from Chart 30.

The cushion is a real conversation piece. Another Janlynn product, the square centre panel is 14-count Aida embroidered with two strands and contains a sentiment from Chart 100 with which every cat-lover must empathise. Two home-loving cats from Chart 108 illustrate the point. The hearts are on Chart 119.

A mini sampler is copied straight from Chart 97, embroidered with two strands on a 3¾in (9.5cm) wide Aida band, and fixed to wooden rods to make an attractive bell-pull wall decoration. The 54-stitch wide band's scalloped edge is available self-coloured, or in a range of contrasting colours. Val's door finger plate from Framecraft is embroidered with two strands of cotton (floss) on 14-count Aida. The alphabet garlanded with lilac and blue flowers is on Charts 51 and 52.

Embroidered on 16-count Aida, the alphabet and border from Chart 54 fit perfectly into the oval frame of this soft cover address book, in which the embroidery is mounted just like a greetings card.

Fridge magnets make useful reminders. This one is worked on 14-count Aida and gets its heartfelt message across loud and clear with three strands of cotton (floss) – only the 'and' is stitched with two strands. The alphabets are from Charts 94, 123 and 124. No excuse to forget anything if there's a useful note block near at hand. The advice is worked on 16-count Aida from Charts 8 and 15, using two strands of cotton (floss). Then the completed embroidery is slipped between the clear sides of the box.

A DAVID & CHARLES BOOK

First published in the UK in 1998

Designs and charts Copyright © Julie Hasler 1998
Text Copyright © Valerie Janitch 1998
Photography and layout Copyright © David & Charles 1998

Julie Hasler has asserted her right to be identified as author of this work in accordance with the Copyright, Designs and Patents Act, 1988.

A catalogue record for this book is available from the British Library.

ISBN 0 7153 0610 3

Photography by Di Lewis
Book design by Malcolm Couch
Printed in the United States
for David & Charles
Brunel House   Newton Abbot   Devon

CONTENTS

INTRODUCTION

I f this is your first venture into cross stitch, or you are still thinking about it, alphabets are an excellent way to start. One 'initial' exercise is all that's needed to act as a passport to the wonderful world of cross stitch embroidery! In fact, a few centuries ago, children used to *learn* their alphabet by cross stitching it onto a sampler. Once they had mastered reading and writing, they would progress to stitching a short prayer or verse, praising the Lord for all his gifts, or beseeching the angels to care for a dear departed parent.

Thankfully, cross stitch is no longer so morbid! It has adopted a decidedly more cheerful image – as you can see from the amazing collection of alphabets charted in this book, which range from the ever-popular romantic florals through gothic, formal, fantasy and humorous, to designs specially for the loved ones and children in your life and, needless to say, Christmas.

A glance at the photographs will show why alphabets are such an ideal introduction to cross stitch. An initialled luggage tag, key ring or bookmark are all quick, easy and fun to embroider. They are also practical forms of identification, proving that this is not just an enjoyable pastime – it's useful, too.

Eventually, of course, you will be inspired to start work on everybody's ultimate ambition, a personal sampler. Sampler enthusiasts are spoilt for choice in these pages. Julie Hasler, with her popular combination of artistry, imagination and wit, has devised large and small, straight-forward and ornate alphabets, with simple backstitch scripts for detailed messages and captions. Whether you are looking to circle a loved one's initial in a bower of roses, or use a bold, contemporary display, this is a book you will enjoy and keep by you for years to come.

An Old-Fashioned Dressing Table
This traditional dressing table has a positively Victorian sense of nostalgia. The period note is set by Framecraft's silver hairbrush, mirror and comb, embroidered with flowing initials from Chart 16. The mirror and brush are identical in shape, but different sizes: so the design was worked with two strands on 16-count Aida for the mirror and 18-count for the brush.
The silver trinket box is from the same collection. The lid is inset with embroidery from Chart 77, worked with two strands over two threads of DMC Belfast 32-count evenweave linen in Dusky Pink. The Victorian theme is again echoed in the oval pincushion, made around a simple cardboard foundation from the same Belfast fabric, this time in Twilight Blue. The true-to-period lettering is from the alphabet on Chart 69. Janlynn's lace-edged sachet – here filled with rose petal pot-pourri – is ready to embroider with two strands on 14-count Aida. The lettering from Chart 12 is bordered with more roses from Chart 78.
No Victorian lady's dressing table would be complete without a dainty pendant. This one, in silver – again from Framecraft – is exquisitely embroidered with a single strand of cotton (floss) over one thread of a 27-count evenweave by Zweigart. The design is from Chart 60.

1

PLANNING AND PREPARING YOUR LETTERING

Planning ahead is vital when cross stitching any kind of alphabet – whether it be a letter, a word, a date or a phrase. An important part of this planning is the use of graph paper, which is as crucial as the fabric you are going to stitch on.

WHERE TO BEGIN

You need two sheets of graph paper. One is the master copy, your whole working chart for the finished embroidery. The other is for copying out individual elements of the design. The example given on the following pages explains the steps to follow.

To embroider the initialled luggage tag shown on page 22, first measure your tag. The one I have chosen is $1^3/_4$ x $2^3/_4$in (4.5 x 7cm) and this represents the maximum area for your design.

To find the number of squares (and thus stitches) available for your design, multiply the actual measurement of your finished piece (in inches) by the number of blocks the fabric has to the inch (2.5cm). If, for example, you are using 14-count Aida, this will be as follows:

$1^3/_4$in (1.75) x 14 = 24
$2^3/_4$in (2.75) x 14 = 38

Therefore the maximum area available for your design is 24 x 38 stitches. Rule out a frame 24 x 38 squares on the first sheet of graph paper.

Neat Deskwork
Positioning the letters to fit the address book (see Chart 100 for the lettering and Chart 12 for the floral spray) and the large wooden trinket box (see Chart 60 for the lettering and Chart 77 for the rose 'fillers') is explained fully on the next few pages.

Heavy glass paperweights are essential aids for the tidy desk, and in this case, to good organisation, too. The IN and OUT are worked on 16-count Aida from Chart 69 and the embroidery is sealed into the recessed base with a protective felt backing.

The little round frame on an (optional) easel adds an elegant touch. The initial from Chart 23 is embroidered with two strands over pairs of threads on a 28-count evenweave by Fabric Flair, in a subtle shade called Wood Violet.

The 'Remember' bookmark (see Chart 86) is embroidered on 14-count Aida and folded inside a self-sealing mount. The reversible diary marker is stitched on 14-count perforated paper using three strands of cotton for extra emphasis (see Chart 25).

COPYING THE LETTERS

Go through the charts and choose an alphabet. When you have found one you like, copy those letters you wish to use onto the second sheet of graph paper. There are two ways that you can do this.

❖ Ignoring the colours, use an ordinary pencil to copy each letter, using a series of crosses to represent the stitches (see Fig 1).

Fig 1

When you are ready to start work, use this chart to position each letter, then use the relevant coloured chart in the book to do the actual embroidery.

❖ The second method is to copy the letters out in full colour on the graph paper, exactly as they appear on the page. This way you will be able to work directly from your master copy.

Whichever way you use, when you have finished, carefully cut out each letter, leaving half a blank square all round (see Fig 2).

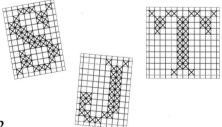

Fig 2

POSITIONING THE LETTERS

To position the letters you will need some plastic adhesive (Blu-Tack) and either Scotch tape or a glue stick.

Place the cut-out letters one by one inside the graph paper frame (see Fig 3), fixing them temporarily with a small amount of plastic adhesive. This allows you to move the letters

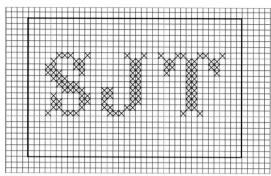

Fig 3

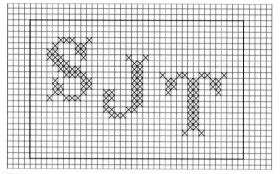

Fig 4

around until you are satisfied with the spacing (see Fig 4). You can then use adhesive tape or a glue stick to fix them permanently into position onto your final piece of graph paper.

ADJUSTING THE FIT

Sometimes the letters you have chosen do not fit well (or at all) within the size of your frame. This is easy to remedy.

Using an example of a different alphabet, say the one on Chart 78, plan to use 14-count Aida again and rule out another frame 24 x 38

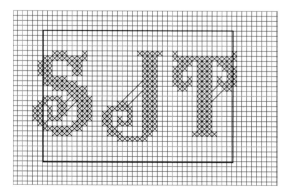

Fig 5

squares. Copy out the initials and cut them up as before and position them on the graph paper. You will see at once that they are too big (see Fig 5). Placing the letters closer together or moving them around only makes them look squashed (see Fig 6).

Fig 6

The answer is to return to your original arrangement (Fig 5) but this time use a 16-count fabric and re-draw the frame according-ly as calculated below:

$$1\tfrac{3}{4}\text{in} \ (1.75) \times 16 = 28$$
$$2\tfrac{3}{4}\text{in} \ (2.75) \times 16 = 44$$

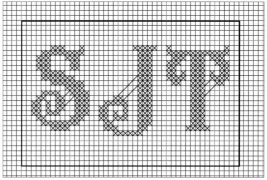

Fig 7

The frame can now be redrawn to 28 x 44 squares and the chosen letters fit comfortably within this space (see Fig 7).

Time for Tea
The gloriously imaginative alphabet on Charts 71–4 is perfect for this teapot stand. The wooden stand is from the wide range produced by Framecraft Miniatures to enhance your embroidery and give it a practical pur-pose too. The embroidery is worked with two strands of stranded cotton (floss) in Wedgwood blue and white, with navy lettering on a pale sky-blue 16-count Aida, the pots are outlined with a single strand of navy.

SPACING

You can now see how critical spacing is when arranging letters. In general you will find it best to settle on a specific number of spaces between letters and words, perhaps two squares between letters and four between words. But don't worry if you can't stick rigidly to this. Sometimes two letters look too close, or too far apart when they are side by side. A cramped look often occurs when the letter A is placed next to a C, G or J (Fig 8).

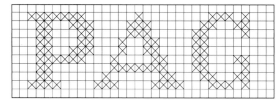

Fig 8

Occasionally more space may be necessary, as with the letter I, which often needs isolating from letters either side (Fig 9).

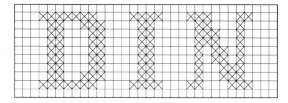

Fig 9

LETTERING IN MORE COMPLEX SHAPES

The same method of designing applies to lettering in more complex shapes. The address book example below shows how to arrange letters within an oval shape.

To mark out a design to fit this oval shape, first measure the oval window frame of your address book in inches vertically and horizontally at its widest points (Fig 10). Mark these on your graph paper, calculated at the fabric count you are planning to use – which in this case might be 16 stitches to the inch (2.5cm) (so each inch equals 16 squares). Then measure the oval window vertically and horizontally at other points and mark these on the graph paper, so that eventually you are able to join up the marks to make a complete oval.

Chose the alphabet you want, in this case the one on Chart 100. Copy out the letters and cut them up as before and position them on the graph paper. You will see that if you place them horizontally that they do not fit (Fig 11). Instead of finding a smaller alphabet, you can re-arrange the letters to follow the oval shape of the frame. Keep re-positioning your letters within the shape, using plastic adhesive until everything is as you want it (Fig 12). You can then fix the letters permanently with tape or a glue stick.

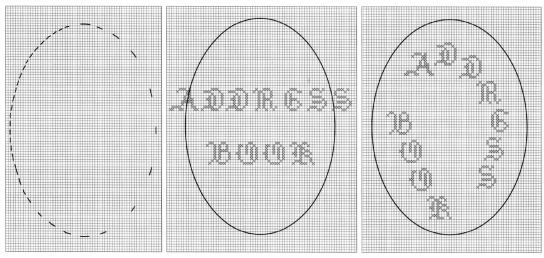

| **Fig 10** | **Fig 11** | **Fig 12** |

ADDING AND ADAPTING DESIGNS

The final address book project photographed on page 2 is a good illustration of how you can add decoration to your lettered design. We have taken the floral spray from Chart 12 and, although it was not quite the right shape, adapted it to fit. Applying the same principle as above, we have copied the part we would like to use, cut it out and snipped bits off until it made an attractive shape that fitted neatly into the design – as shown in the photograph.

For Grandmother with Love

The strong colouring of the cotton frill of this hoop is dramatically echoed in the striking lettering from Chart 60, worked with two strands on the 14-count Aida and outlined with one in a darker shade.

Gran herself may be a dedicated stitcher, and Fabric Flair's calico bag is just the job to keep all her bits and pieces together. Chart 115 provides ideal lettering for the Hardanger band, and Chart 14 reminds Gran to pop her scissors into Janlynn's 14-count Aida sachet. The flowers are from Chart 79.

The 18-count padded top of a tiny pincushion is lettered from Chart 124, while the button box uses Chart 79. The lettering on the heart-shaped porcelain trinket box is backstitched following Chart 123 and the butterflies are from Chart 113.

2
MATERIAL NEEDS

Needles and scissors are the two most important pieces of equipment in your workbasket. Cross stitch is worked with a small blunt tapestry needle (size 24 or 26). Have several of these needles and take good care of them by keeping them in a special pincushion or a needlecase. When pins are needed they should be fine and sharp.

Two pairs of scissors are necessary. You will need a large pair to cut the fabric and a small pair of embroidery scissors to cut your threads. Both should be sharp and well aligned. Sharpen them regularly – an electric knife and scissors grinder does the job quickly and very efficiently. A separate pair of scissors reserved for cutting paper is an advantage. Occasionally, you will need to cut up paper for charts and this tends to blunt scissors very quickly.

Although cross stitch may be worked in the hand, to ensure a perfectly smooth and even finish the fabric should be stretched taut. You can achieve this easily with an embroidery hoop. Choose a 4in (10cm), 5in (12.5cm) or 6in (15cm) diameter plastic or wooden hoop, with a screw-type tension adjuster. Larger pieces of embroidery should be worked on a frame. Ask your local needlecraft shop to show you a selection, and advise you.

CHART-MAKING EQUIPMENT

As mentioned in Chapter 1, a pad of graph paper is essential. This does not need to be an expensive one from a special shop; you can get it from any ordinary stationers. It can be imperial or metric measure, it doesn't matter, as long as each inch or two centimetres is divided into 10 x 10 tiny squares (like the charts in this book). There is usually also a faint sub-division into 5 x 5 tiny squares. The bolder lines are a great help, both when you are copying out charts, and when you are working the design. When you copy out a design, always follow the heavy lines on the original chart, as this prevents mistakes.

Have a well-sharpened fairly soft pencil (HB or B) and a soft eraser (for the inevitable odd mistake!), a ruler and something with which to colour the charts. For colouring you can use watercolour paints, coloured pencils or felt-tip pens. All are perfectly good, though you have to take care that watercolours do not run into each other. On balance, pencils or felt-tip pens are probably quicker, but you can get a more accurate representation of colour by mixing paints.

When you are making up a charted design, for a sampler for instance, you will want to stick small pieces of graph paper onto a larger background sheet. Use a dry stick adhesive

Baby Days
A birth sampler recording all the vital details is a must for every new baby, and of course this book is invaluable for that purpose. However, there are plenty of other ways to use alphabets in the nursery. Janlynn are full of practical ideas to embroider on 14-count Aida as shown here. A charming ruffled hoop tells everyone whose room it is, and the letters from Chart 75 worked with two strands pick up the delicate colours of the floral frill. The special message on the Aida hood of the baby towel worked with two strands is composed from the alphabets and motifs on Charts 85 and 114.

A cosy quilted cover to keep a baby's bottle warm is a useful precaution against sleepless nights. The lettering on the central band is from Chart 110, and is worked with two strands outlined with backstitch using one strand in a darker shade. A bib, using Charts 1–7, would make a perfect companion present.

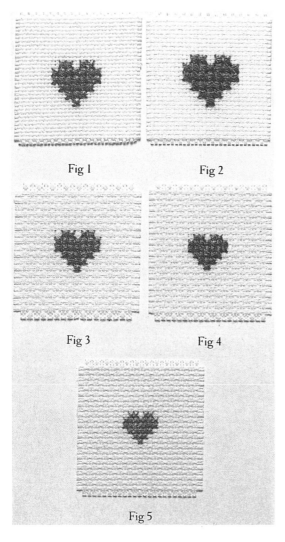

Fig 1

Fig 2

Fig 3

Fig 4

Fig 5

Fig 1 25-count evenweave fabric (Lugana), giving 12½ stitches to the inch (2.5cm), worked with two strands of embroidery cotton (floss)

Fig 2 22-count Hardanger fabric, giving eleven stitches to the inch (2.5cm), worked with three strands of embroidery cotton (floss)

Fig 3 14-count Aida fabric, giving fourteen stitches to the inch (2.5cm), worked with two strands of embroidery cotton (floss)

Fig 4 16-count Aida fabric, giving sixteen stitches to the inch (2.5cm), worked with two strands of embroidery cotton (floss)

Fig 5 18-count Aida fabric, giving eighteen stitches to the inch (2.5cm), worked with one single strand of embroidery cotton (floss)

like UHU Stic, an all-purpose clear adhesive like UHU, or a special transparent mending tape like 3M Magic Scotch tape which has a matt surface so that you can write on it.

FABRICS TO USE

Cross stitch can only be worked over an 'evenweave' fabric. That is to say one where there is exactly the same number of threads to the inch in each direction, so that when you work one cross stitch, the width and depth will be exactly the same. And, when you work a square block of ten cross stitches, the width and depth will again be exactly the same. If the fabric was not exactly evenly woven, it may not be apparent in one stitch – but it would begin to become very obvious on a larger block, which, when stitching was finished, would not be square.

There are various types of evenweave fabrics that you can use. *Aida* is the most popular with cross stitchers. The threads in this are quite fine, and woven in blocks. Each cross stitch is worked over a block of threads. If there are fourteen stitches to the inch, this is called 14-count and will give you fourteen stitches to the inch. Aida bands are also available in several widths, from 1in (2.5cm) to 4in (10cm) and they may have plain, coloured, scalloped or woven borders. These make a

In Safe Keeping
The pale terracotta 14-count Aida by Fabric Flair is a perfect match for the Framecraft porcelain box in which it is set. The initial is from the squirrel alphabet which begins on Chart 32. The smaller box has the squirrel from Chart 38 guarding the coins from Chart 123 and is worked on 16-count Aida.
  The make-up purse is another useful item from Fabric Flair. The strip of Aida is 26 stitches wide, and the two strand lettering comes from Chart 60. The hard-wearing twill 'Big Bag' from Janlynn would make a terrific toy bag, and if a child is keen to have a go, would make an excellent introduction to cross stitch. The top section is 6-count Aida, stitched with the bold alphabet from Charts 107–8, using a full six strands of space-dyed embroidery cotton. Here the lettering is outlined in three strand backstitch, but it isn't essential.

quick and easy decoration when appliquéd to towels, garments and soft furnishings. They are ideal for curtain tie-backs, and make an attractive band for a straw hat, too. Simply cut the required length of band, and then repeat your embroidered design along it.

Also available is *evenweave linen*, *cotton* and *cotton blends* of mixed fibres. Here the weave is more conventional, and the threads are single. In this case, each stitch is worked over two threads in each direction. So this time a 28-count fabric will give you fourteen stitches to the inch.

Finally there is *Hardanger*, which is between Aida and linen. It is woven with pairs of finer threads, and a cross stitch should usually cover two pairs of threads in each direction. However, for very fine work, the stitch may be worked over a single pair of threads in each direction.

You will also find *waste canvas* very useful. This allows you to embroider on fabrics where cross stitch would not normally be possible because there are no evenweave threads to

Lunch in the Country

The Country Cottage table linens range from Janlynn is attractive and practical. Looking just like natural linen, it is in fact machine washable polycotton. The fabric is a 19-count evenweave, so the place mat and napkin are embroidered with three strands of cotton (floss) over pairs of threads, then backstitched with one strand. Chart 45 provides a country garden design for the place mat, and the napkin uses a butterfly alphabet from Chart 76. The initial is repeated in the Framecraft serviette holder, this time embroidered on Fabric Flair's pure linen evenweave, which has 31 threads to the inch.

Three tiny butterflies have escaped from Chart 76 to decorate the place card: another attractive item from the Framecraft collection.

Send a Card

Cards are undoubtedly the favourite application for cross stitch. A greetings card is always appreciated, but how much more so when it is personally hand-stitched for the recipient.

DMC produce a wide range of 'Keepsake Cards', a few of which are shown here. The cards provide a charming pictorial mount for a simple piece of embroidery when you are short of time, and the wide range of designs includes something suitable for almost everyone and every occasion.

follow. Simply tack (baste) the plain white canvas over the area you wish to embroider – work the cross stitch over the canvas and through the fabric.

When the embroidery is finished, place it face up on a thick folded towel. Dip a sponge in clean, warm water and squeeze it out, not too hard. Then dab it firmly all over the embroidered canvas, including the outer edges, making the work very damp. Allow a few minutes for the water to soak in and do its work, then very carefully draw out the threads, one at a time, using a pair of tweezers.

Waste canvas is 27in (68cm) wide, and comes in mesh sizes 8/9, 10, 12 and 14, giving eight/nine, ten, twelve and fourteen stitches to the inch respectively.

THREADS TO USE

You will find an interesting variety of threads at your needlecraft shop, but all the examples in this book are worked with stranded embroidery cotton (floss), which is generally considered the most satisfactory for this type of cross stitch. DMC six-strand embroidery cottons (floss) come in a truly magnificent range of colours, which means that they offer breathtaking shading effects.

In use, the strands are separated. The number that you use depends on the fabric – the smaller your crosses, the fewer strands you will need. Two or three strands are the most usual: use two strands for twelve or more stitches to the inch (2.5cm) and three strands for eleven or less stitches to the inch (2.5cm). For very fine work, use only one strand.

· 3 ·
BEGINNING THE EMBROIDERY

Before you begin to work the embroidery of your chosen design prevent the cut edges of your fabric fraying by either whip-stitching or machine-stitching all round. Alternatively, turn under and tack a small hem.

WHERE TO START

First find the centre points of the chart and your fabric. If you begin stitching from the centre, you can be sure that your design will be correctly positioned. If you want your design

to be placed off-centre on the fabric you will need to find the centre of the design itself, but you can still follow the method given below.

To find the centre point of the chart, place a ruler horizontally across the middle, and measure and mark the centre of the design itself with a tiny line. Then place your ruler vertically over the design and do the same thing – making a small cross (+). The centre of the cross is the centre of your chart. Alternatively, you can count the squares in each direction and divide the number in half to find the centre.

To find the centre point of the fabric, fold it in half and crease. Fold it in the other direction and crease the fold again. Make a line of tacking (basting) stitches in contrasting cotton along each fold, following the woven threads. The point where the lines cross is the equivalent to the cross (+) on your chart.

Sometimes it is not practical to start stitching at the centre. In this case, count the number of squares or stitches from the centre of the chart to the point where you want to begin, then count the same number of blocks or double threads on your fabric.

GETTING READY

Cut off the required amount of cotton (floss): 18–20in (45–50cm) is a comfortable length to work with. One at a time, draw out the number of strands you require. If working on a 14-count fabric, you will need two strands. Then put the individual strands together again: always do this, as it ensures a neat, full stitch which covers the block properly.

Thread the needle, but never make a knot! Knots create bumps at the back of your work, and spoil the smooth surface of the embroidery. Instead, weave the tail ends of the thread – at the beginning and end of each bit of embroidery – through the back of existing stitches (see Figs 4 and 9 on page 23). Place the remaining strands in a thread holder.

If you are using an embroidery hoop allow approximately 2½in (6cm) more fabric than the size of the outer ring of the hoop all round. To place the fabric in the hoop, rest the area to be embroidered over the inner ring and carefully push the outer ring down over it. Pull the fabric gently and evenly, making sure that it is drum taut in the hoop, and that the weave is straight, tightening the screw adjuster as you do so.

When working, you will find it best to have the screw in the 'ten o'clock' position, as this will prevent the thread becoming tangled with the screw as you stitch. If you are left-handed, have the screw in the 'one o'clock' position. As you work, re-tighten the fabric every so often, to keep it taut.

STARTING TO CROSS STITCH

All the designs are worked with full cross stitches, although occasionally a half cross is used (forming a triangle, instead of a square). Sometimes a design is outlined in backstitch, which gives it added emphasis. Backstitching can also be used to pick out detail. The only other stitch which appears is a French knot, which is sometimes used for eyes, etc.

As previously explained, the cross is usually worked over a complete block of an Aida fabric; over two threads in each direction of an evenweave linen or cotton; and over two pairs of threads of a Hardanger fabric. If your design incorporates half crosses, you will find it easier to stitch on a fabric where you work over pairs of threads, rather than solid blocks.

Man About the House
The red note block is stitched with two strands of cotton (floss) on 16-count Aida. The paperweights feature the DIY alphabet on Chart 63, worked with two strands on 14-count Aida, while the frosted glass trinket box is from Chart 38 on 14-count Aida.

Father's rule is worked on 14-count Aida using two strands and one for the detail, using the alphabet on Chart 120. Both key rings are from Chart 123 – the car key on 14-count Aida, and the garage key on 16-count, both with two strands.

The bookmark backstitch lettering from Chart 123 is stitched on 26-stitch 2in (5cm) wide Aida band with two strands. A second bookmark uses the alphabet on Chart 109, on 14-count Aida using three strands of red outlined with one of black.

Going Out

The mirror, spectacles case and key ring are all from the Framecraft range and each is monogrammed with the initial from three different alphabets (Charts 23, 75 and 80). The 14-count sachet, from Janlynn, is embroidered in space-dyed cottons using the alphabet from Chart 100. A few extra lines of cross stitch in the same threads follow the shape of the bag to form a simple decoration which complements the lettering. All the colours are twisted to make the cord which ties the bag securely. A stitched invitation provides a lasting memento. For one, an unusual silver flecked 28-count evenweave from Fabric Flair has been used. The letters are from Chart 124 using two strands of stranded cotton (floss) over pairs of thread. In the other, the wording from Chart 124 is backstitched with a single strand of cotton (floss) on 14-count Aida, introduced with a capital letter from Chart 50.

To begin the first stitch, bring the needle up from the wrong side, through a hole in the fabric at the left-hand corner of the stitch (Fig 1); leave a short length underneath and weave it neatly through the backs of the first few stitches, once you have made them (Fig 2).

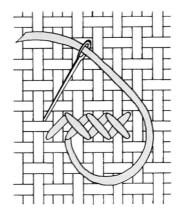

Fig 4

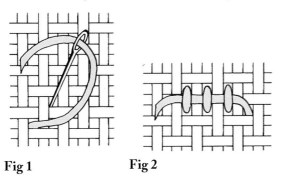

Fig 1   **Fig 2**

To work an individual or isolated cross stitch bring the needle diagonally up across the pairs of threads or block that you want to cover, and take it down through the hole at the right-hand corner (Fig 1). This is the first half of your stitch. The needle is now at the back of the fabric. Take the thread straight down and bring your needle up through the bottom right-hand hole (Fig 3): then take the thread diagonally across and up to the remaining corner at the top left, pushing the needle down through it (Fig 3). Your cross stitch is now complete.

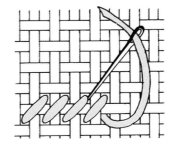

Fig 5

Fig 6

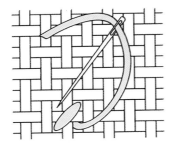

Fig 3

If you have a horizontal row of stitches in the same colour, work the first half of all the stitches across the line (Fig 4): then return and complete the crosses (Fig 5). Work vertical rows of stitches in the same way (Fig 6). To make a triangular stitch, filling only half a square, push your needle through the *centre* of the block to form a three-quarter stitch (Fig 7).

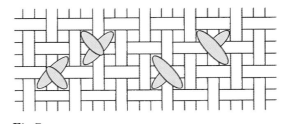

Fig 7

Finish off your thread on the wrong side, by running your needle under the backs of four or more stitches.

NOTE: Each vertical and horizontal thread on Figs 1–7 represents a *block* of threads on Aida fabric; a *pair* of threads on evenweave linen; or *two pairs* of threads on Hardanger fabric.

FRENCH KNOTS

These stitches are ideal for adding small features to designs, such as animal eyes and noses. To make a French knot bring the needle up from the wrong side and wind the thread around it twice. Push the needle down through the fabric one thread, or part of a block, away from the starting point to finish (Fig 8).

Always work the backstitch after all the cross-stitch embroidery is finished, using one strand less than you used for the cross stitch.

Backstitch is worked from hole to hole, following the same blocks as the cross stitches, and can be stitched in vertical, horizontal or diagonal lines, as Fig 9. Take care not to pull the stitches too tight, or the contrast of colour will be lost. Begin and finish off as for cross stitch.

Fig 8

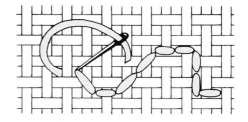

Fig 9

OUTLINING AND DETAILING IN BACKSTITCH

Some of the designs are outlined with backstitch to give them greater clarity or emphasis. Backstitch is also used to pick out fine details.

SOME HINTS AND TIPS

It is important to keep your tension even so the fabric will be pulled out of shape. If you are worried about this happening, use a hoop, as described earlier in this chapter. Work each stitch by pushing your needle straight up through the fabric, and then straight down again, keeping the fabric smooth and taut. There should be no slack, but don't pull the thread too tight – draw it through so that it lies snug and flat.

Do not carry threads across the back of an open expanse of fabric. If you are working separate areas of the same colour, finish off and begin again. Loose threads, especially dark colours, will be visible from the right side of your work when the project is finished. If the thread becomes twisted while you are working, drop the needle and let it hang down freely. It will untwist itself. Don't continue working with twisted thread, as it will appear thinner, and won't cover the fabric satisfactorily.

Never leave the needle in the design area of work between embroidery sessions. Not only might it distort the fabric, but it could rust if left for any length of time, and leave a mark.

Taking a Break
Cross stitch comes in very useful for those vacation requisites. The very simple luggage tag in black on khaki 14-count Aida is from Chart 25. The elegant citrus green initials are worked with two strands sharply outlined with one of black, from Chart 77 and 78, are on dark grey 16-count Aida. Simply cut your finished embroidery to size, then snap it into Framecraft's clear plastic frame.

A beach bag is a priority when going to the seaside. Janlynn's 'Not-so-little Tote' is 14-count Aida, and the alphabet on Chart 65 couldn't be more suitable. Stitched with two strands of cotton (floss), the motifs are outlined with one strand of very dark brown. Don't forget to take a book and cross stitch a bookmark so you won't lose your place. The distinctive lettering from Chart 13 complements the deep lace edge, which might have been designed for the romantic blockbuster. Your sunglasses or spectacles will be safe in this pretty case with the initial in a circlet of roses from Chart 78. Both these are worked with two strands on 18-count Aida, from Framecraft.

4

FINISHING TECHNIQUES

The first thing you must do when you have completed your embroidery is to press it. You will be surprised how professional your work looks afterwards. Fold a thick towel and place the fabric right-side down on it. Then cover the back with a thin, thoroughly damp cloth and press evenly and gently. Leave the embroidery until it is cool and dry.

BACKING PICTURES

Whether or not you plan to frame a picture or sampler, it will need to be mounted on a firm backing. You can buy a self-adhesive board which is specially made for this purpose, or you can use an ordinary acid-free stiff mounting board or foam board (available from artists' suppliers).

Cut a piece of board exactly the size of the finished design. Trim at least 2in (5cm) of the fabric all round the design. You can allow less – 1¼in (3cm) – on smaller pieces, but for larger items, it is wise to allow a greater amount.

There are two ways to fix the overlapping fabric round the edges of the board: you can either oversew it to the edges, or lace it across the back. In each case, place the embroidery face up on the board, positioned so that the edges of the design are exactly level with the edges of the board. To do this, mark all round the edge of the design with a tacking (basting) thread, then pin the fabric carefully to the edge of the board, matching the centres on each side before working outwards to the four corners with your pins. Then mitre the corners as shown in Fig 1.

To hold the fabric in place, either oversew neatly all round the edge or use strong linen

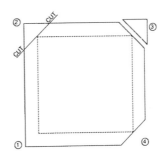

Fig 1

thread to lace together with long stitches the two opposite edges of the surplus fabric, first the top and bottom (Fig 2), and then the two sides in the same way, across the first set of lacing stitches. Seal the corners with a smear of clear adhesive, such as UHU, to prevent them fraying.

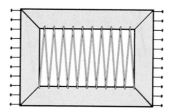

Fig 2

For very small pieces, you can use double-sided tape to hold the surplus fabric down at the back. Finish off the cut edges by taping over them with a transparent mending tape.

If the picture or sampler is not to be framed, finish off the back neatly by cutting a piece of cartridge paper, or felt, slightly smaller than the finished project. Then fix it over the back with clear adhesive or double-sided tape.

WONDER PRODUCTS

There are three products which offer enormous potential when making up cross-stitch projects. *Vilene* is a non-woven interlining material that is widely used in dressmaking to interline, reinforce or stiffen garments. It comes in a range of weights. All weights are sew-in, but some are iron-on as well – in which case, place the bonded side over the back of the fabric, with a damp cloth on top – and a hot iron will fuse the Vilene to the fabric.

Vilene Bondaweb and *Wundaweb* both look like ordinary Vilene interlining, but they are bonded on *both* sides, allowing one piece of fabric to be fused to another. Bondaweb is paper-backed: when cut to the required size, place the bonded material on the back of one piece of fabric and iron over the paper. When it has cooled, peel the paper away, place the wrong side of the second piece of fabric on top, and iron it into place, using a damp cloth. Wundaweb looks like a tape made from the finest Vilene, and is used to make hems without stitching. The raw edge of the fabric is turned over to the wrong side, the Wundaweb 'tape' is placed between the layers of fabric and the hem is ironed under a damp cloth, when it will become permanently fused together.

CLEANING AND CARING FOR YOUR CROSS STITCH

Cross-stitch embroideries worked on cotton or linen fabrics may be laundered quite safely, if handled with care. For the treatment of work using their stranded embroidery cotton (floss), DMC suggest washing in soapy, warm water. Squeeze without twisting, and hang to dry. Iron the reverse side, using two layers of white linen or cotton. Always wash embroidery separately from your other laundry. Avoid dry cleaning.

Off to School
A colourful array of projects to stitch for schoolchildren include Janlynn's 'Lil' Tote' bag, Framecraft rulers, and smart luggage tags.

  Homework is a bit more bearable when the place is marked with a strip of Mill Hill 14-count perforated paper, lettered with three strands of space-dyed thread using Chart 25. This encouraging piece of moral support is quick to stitch in bright colours on 14-count Aida: it comes from Charts 8 and 123 and is mounted in a DMC Chelsea Studio card.

ACKNOWLEDGEMENTS

I would like to thank Maxine Steinberg for doing so much of the embroidery for this book – and for doing it so beautifully.

Thanks also to my suppliers: H.W. Peel & Co. Ltd, Norwester House, Fairway Drive, Greenford, Middlesex, UB6 8PW (for graph paper); DMC Creative World Ltd (and Adam Wyles), Pullman Road, Wigston, Leicester, LE8 2DY (for Aida and evenweave fabrics, stranded cottons and metallic threads, Aida bands, Keepsake cards and Chelsea Studio cards); Framecraft Miniatures Ltd, 372–376 Summer Lane, Hockley, Birmingham, B19 3QA (for bell-pulls, trinket boxes, pincushions, paperweights, coaster, fridge magnets, luggage tags, rulers, bookmarks, wooden teapot stand, jar lacies, miniature brass frame and easel, key rings, serviette holders, door finger plate, handbag mirror, spectacles cases, address books, jotter note blocks, place card, gift tags, silver-plated dressing table set, clothes brush and jewellery, and Mill Hill perforated paper); Janlynn Corporation, 34 Front Street, PO Box 51848, Indian Orchard, MA 01151-5848, USA (for ruffled hoops, baby bibs, bottle warmer and towel, large and small bags and totes, lace-edged sachets, cushion cover, Christmas stockings and Country Cottage table linens); Fabric Flair Ltd, The Old Brewery, The Close, Warminster, Wiltshire BA12 9AL (for Aida and evenweave fabrics, needlework craft bag and make-up purse).

When writing to any suppliers, please include a stamped self-addressed envelope.

(opposite) Traditional Christmas

The snow-capped card uses Chart 21 and 22, 14-count Aida and three strands of cotton (floss) outlined with a single strand of black. 'Christmas' is backstitched from Chart 124 with two strands. 'Noel' is reproduced in two strands of metallic thread from Chart 99. Letters from Charts 56–58 decorate the stockings, boldly stitched on 14-count Aida with three strands.

Made-in-a-moment Gift Cards

An embroidered card makes a gift extra-special. All you have to do is steal a suitable motif from one of the charts, for example the little train is the same as the ones on Charts 89 and 90, with extra backstitch added around the wheels. Work it on a suitable cross stitch count to fit a card, mount it, and your exclusive gift tag is ready to go.

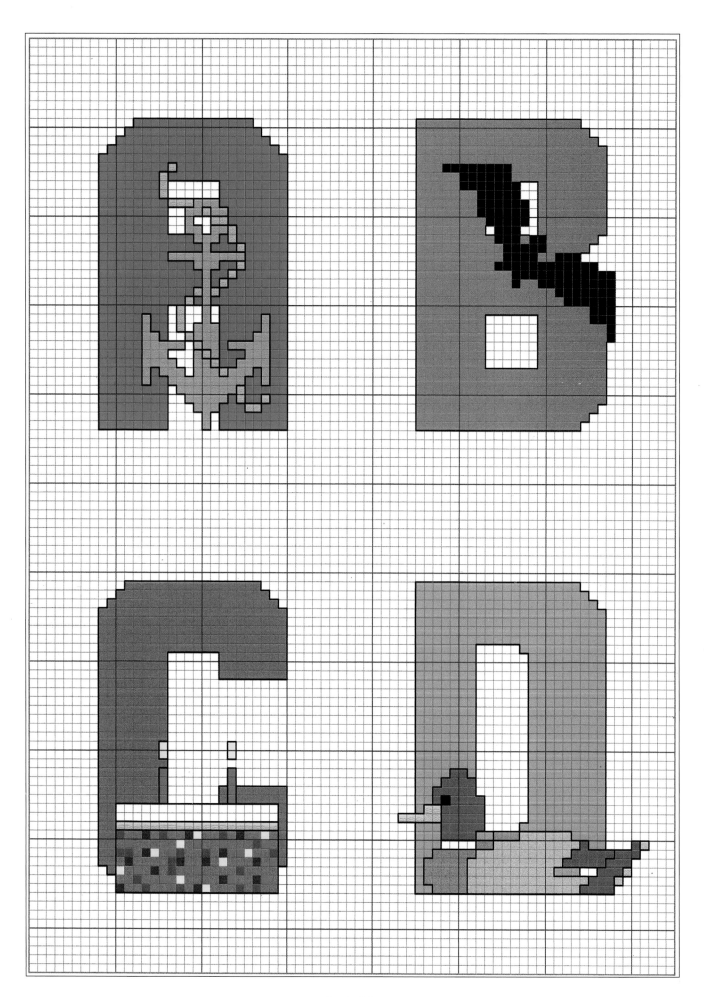

CHART 1

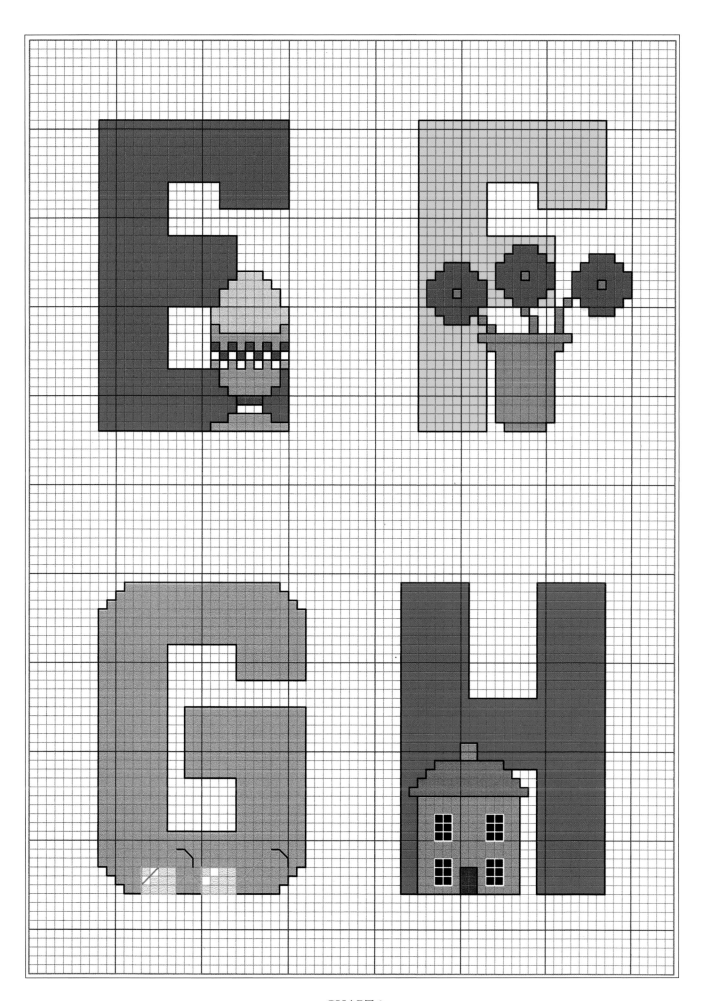

CHART 2

CHART 3

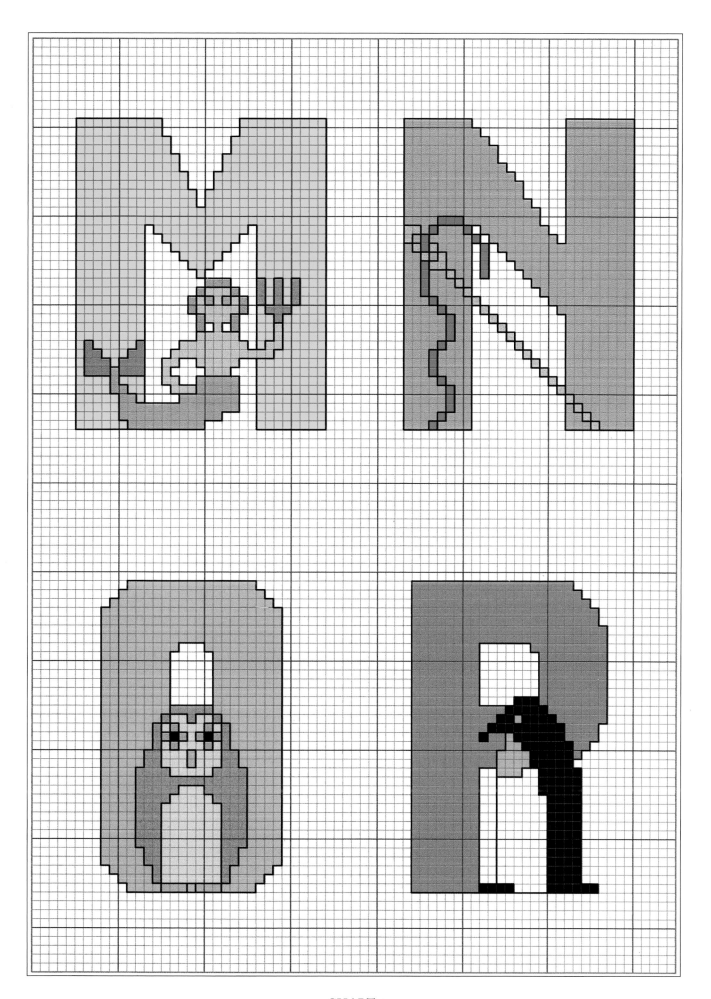

CHART 4

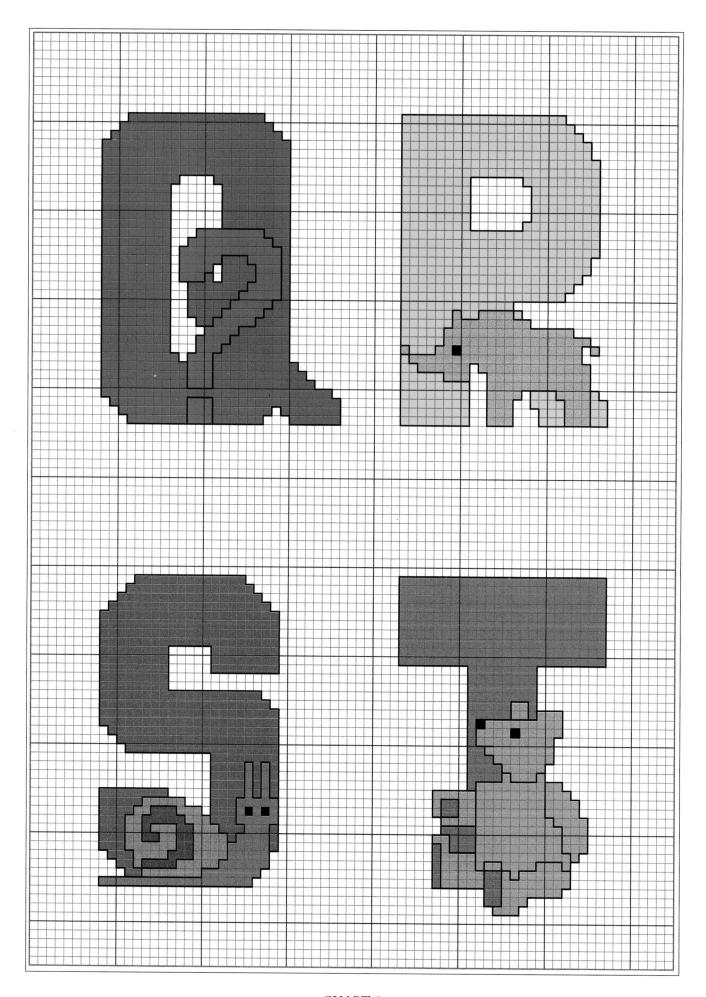

CHART 5

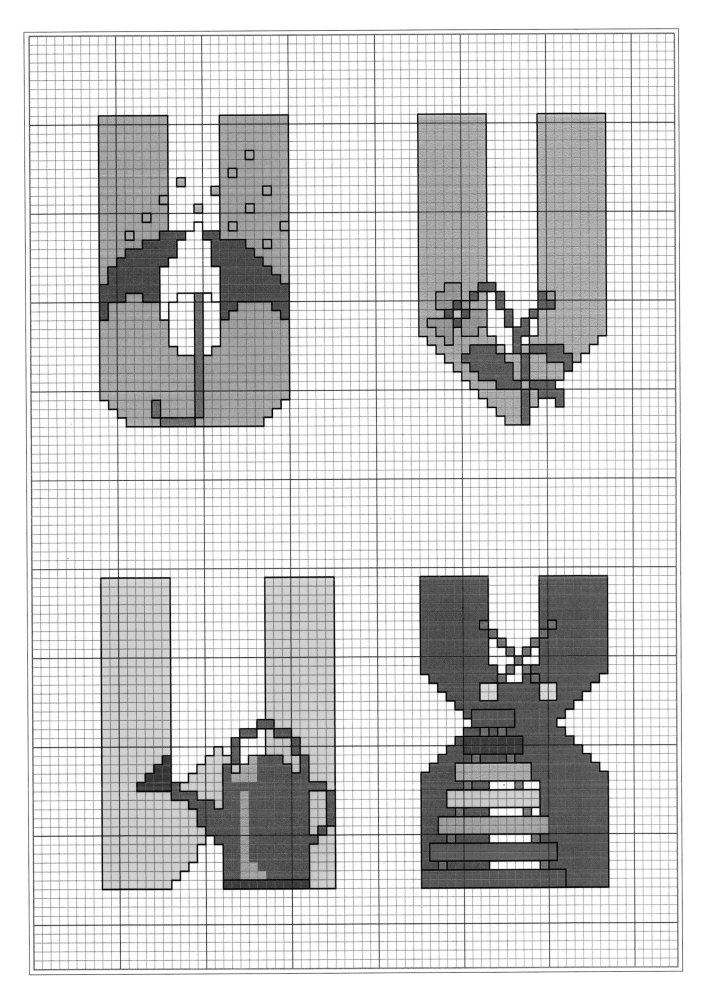

CHART 6

CHART 7

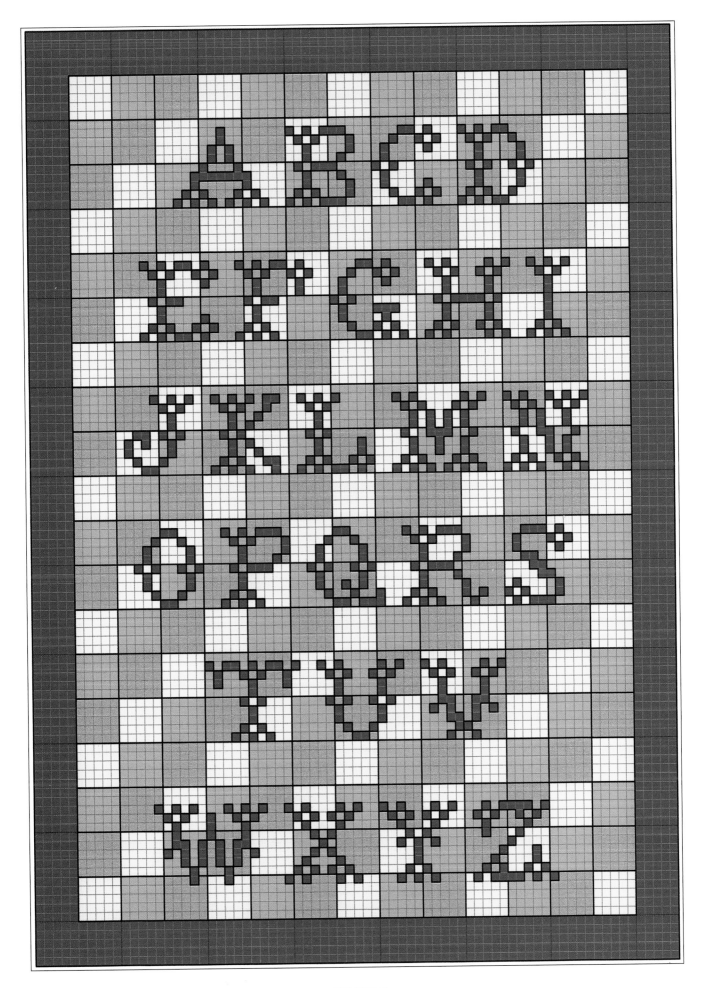

CHART 8

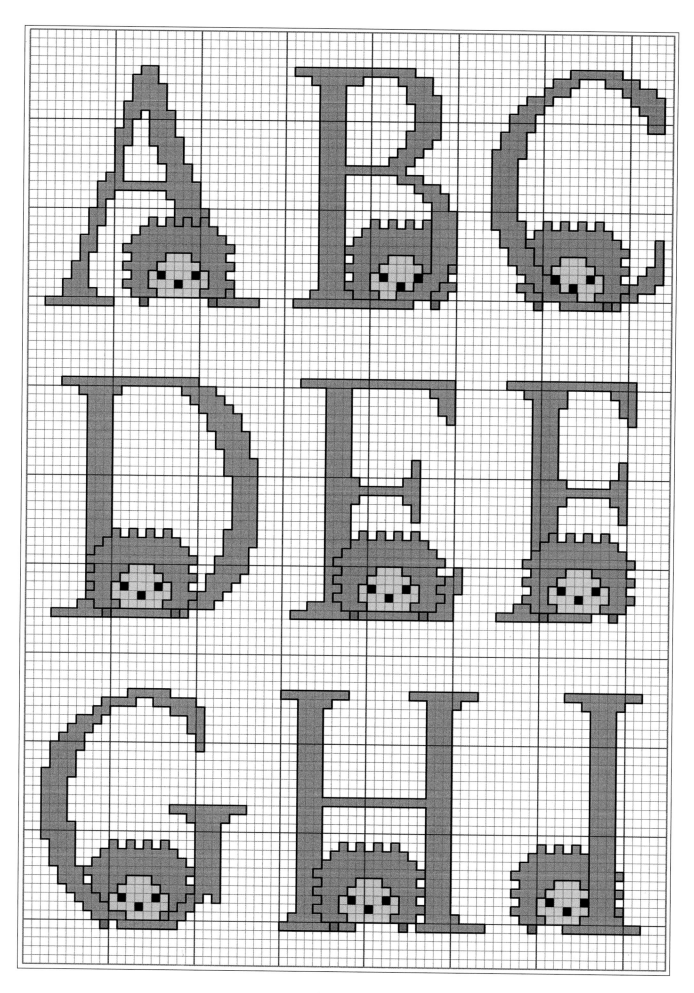

CHART 9

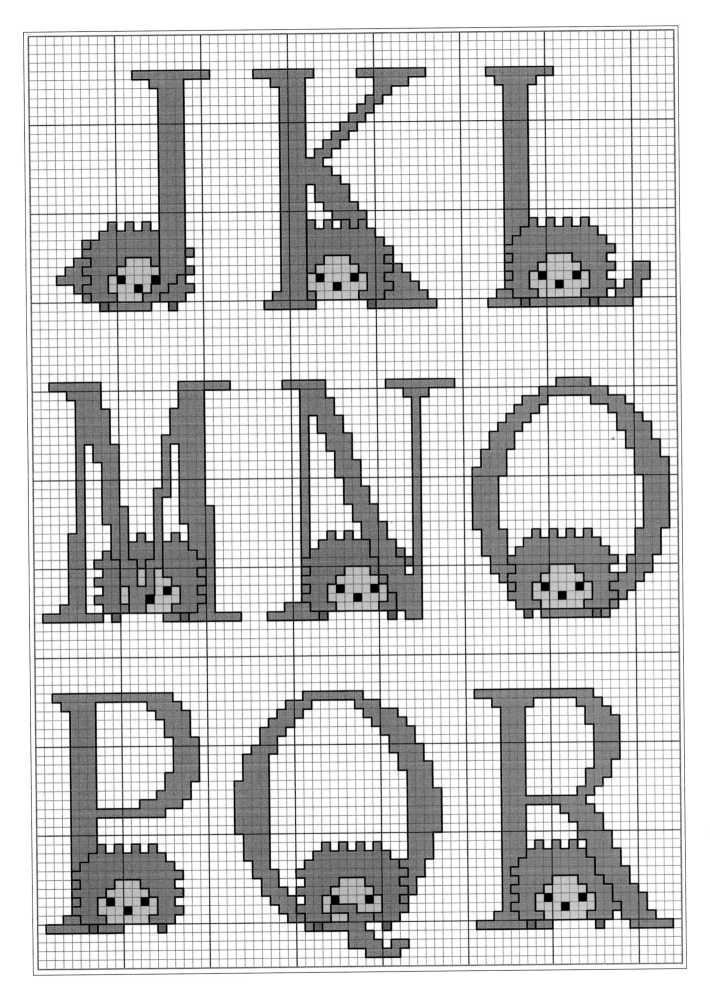

CHART 10

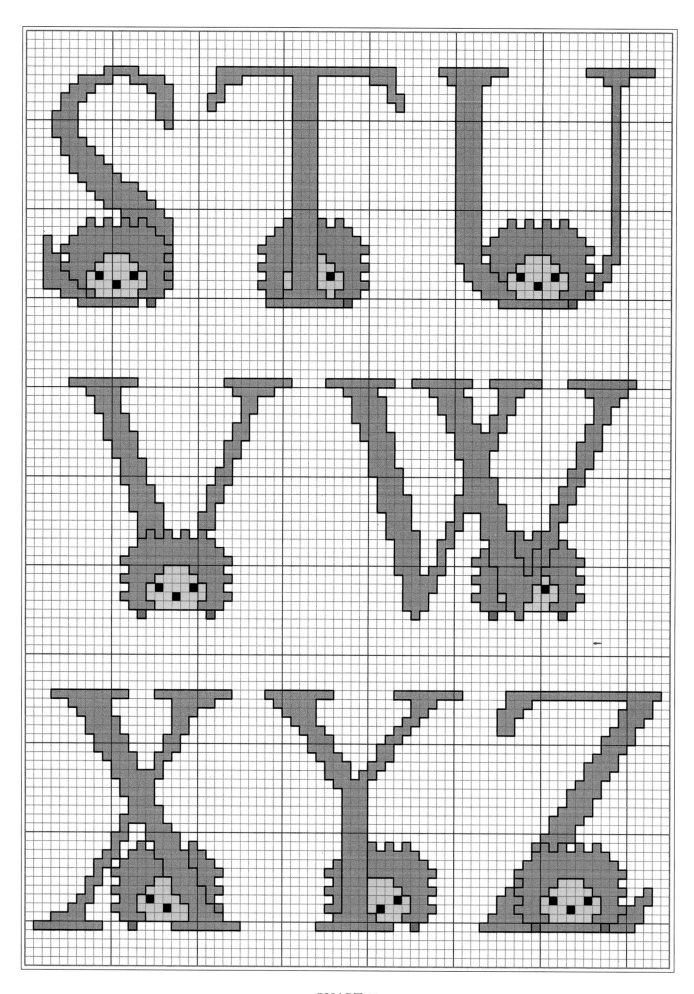

CHART 11

CHART 12

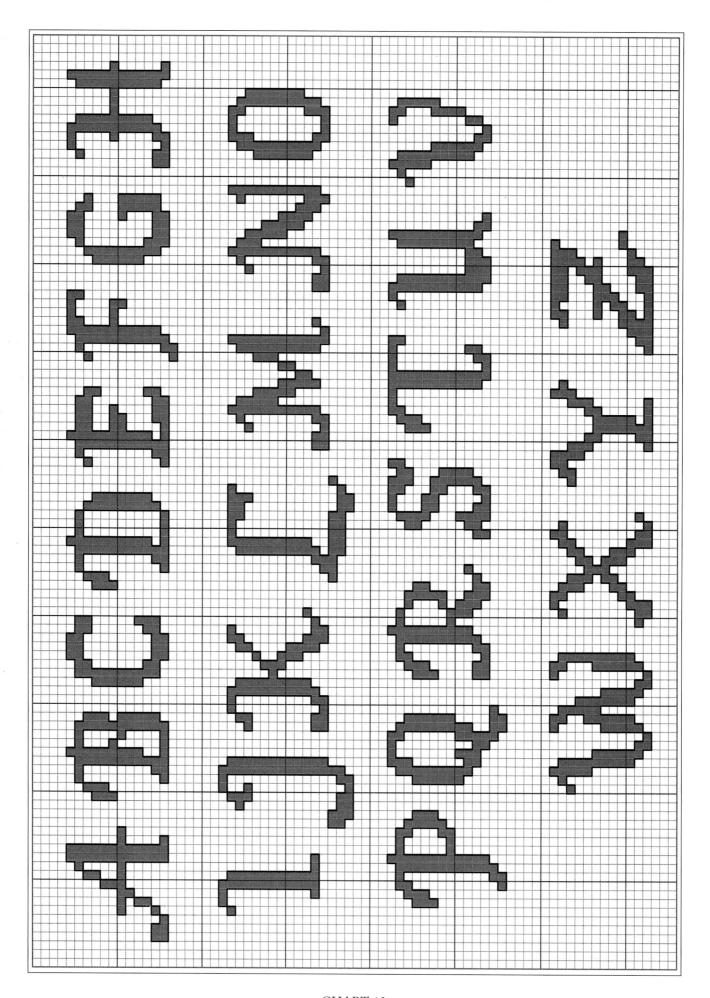

CHART 13

CHART 14

CHART 15

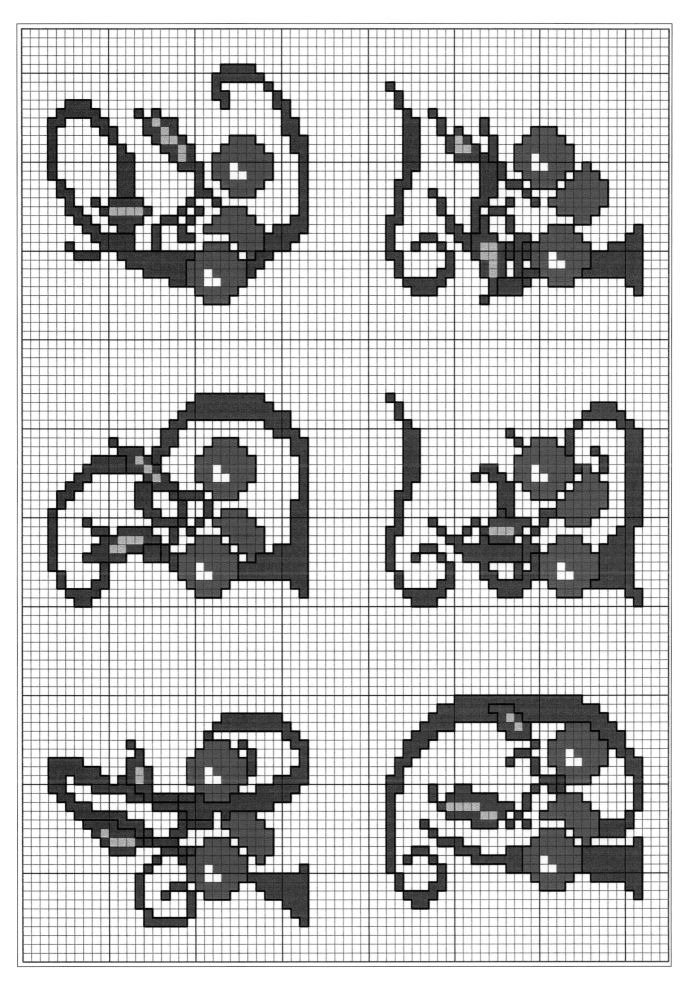

CHART 16

CHART 17

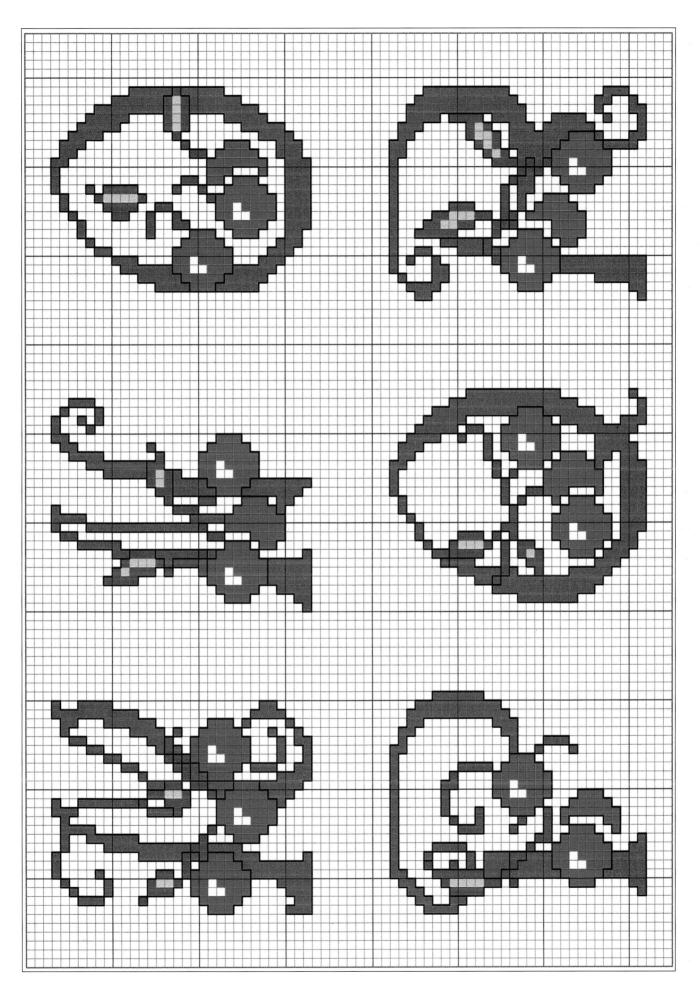

CHART 18

CHART 19

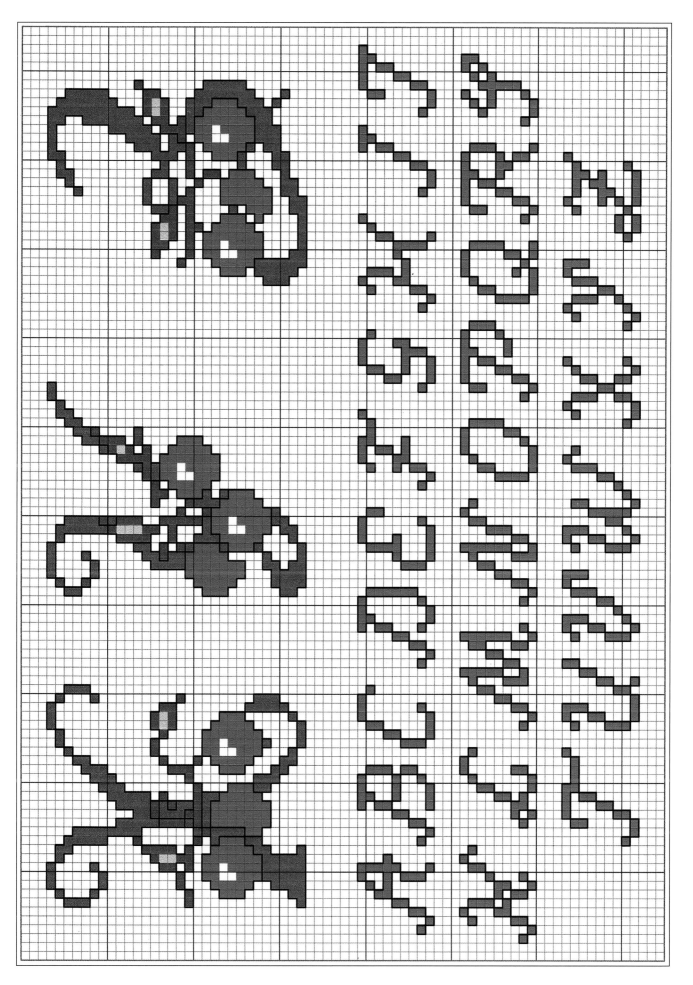

CHART 20

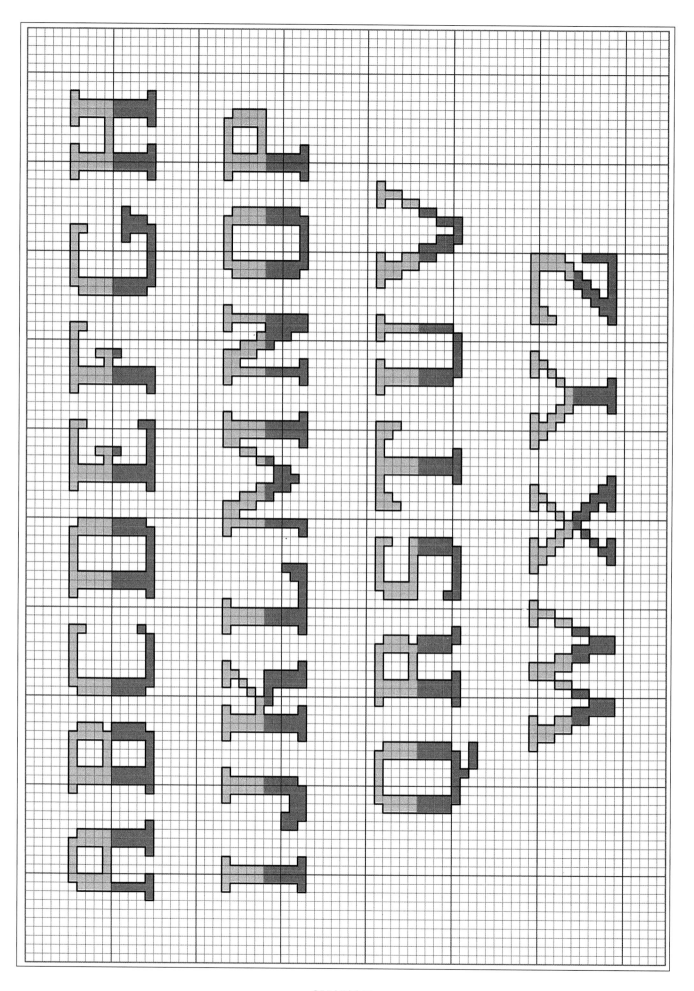

CHART 21

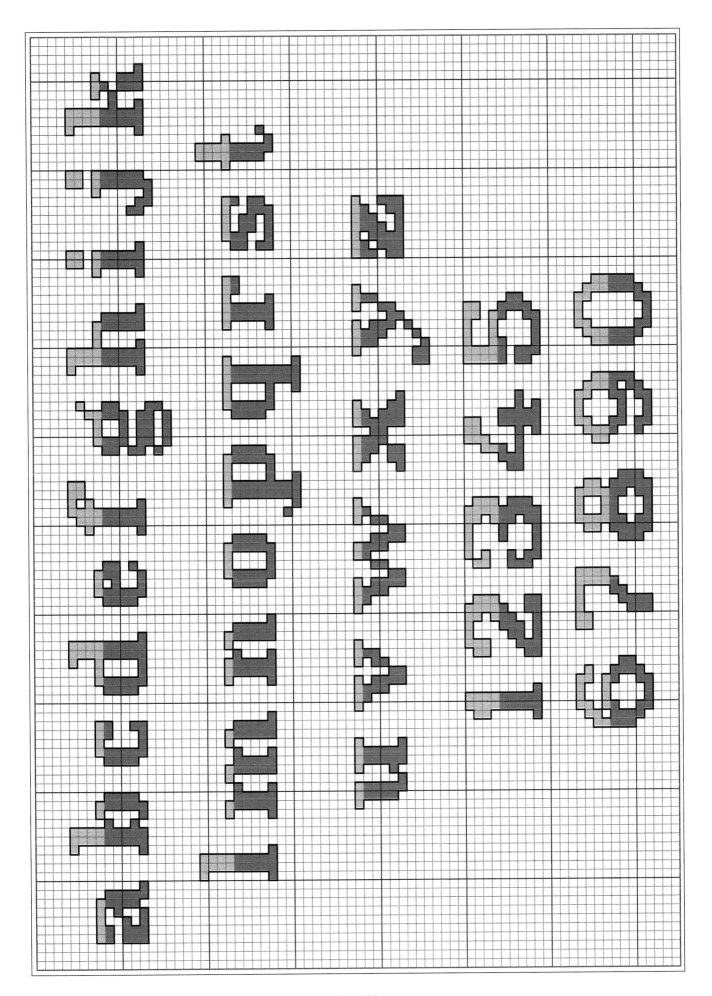

CHART 22

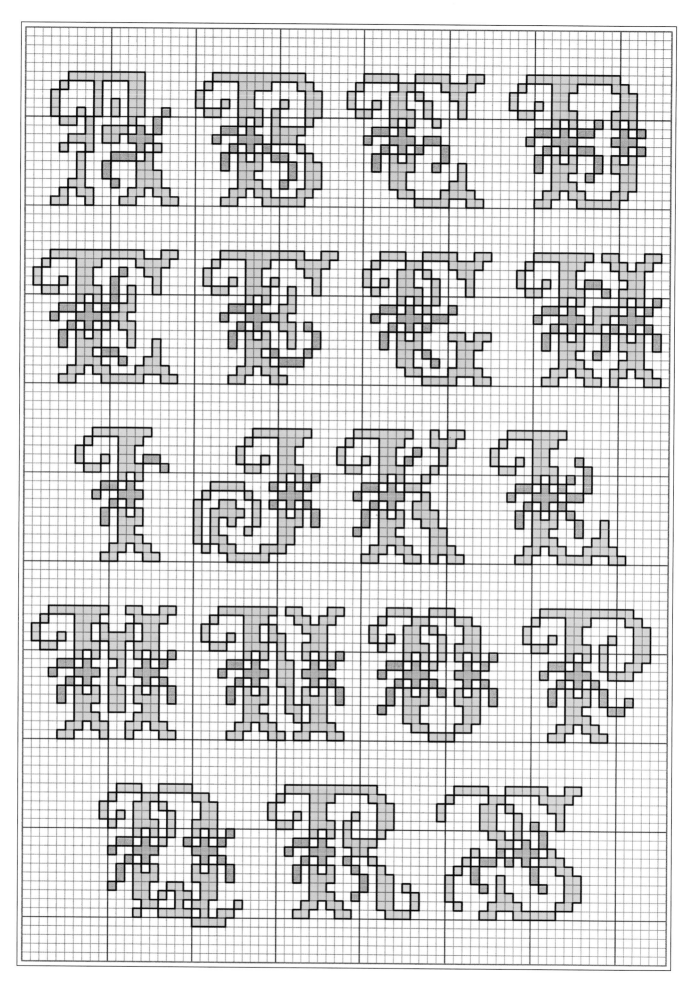

CHART 23

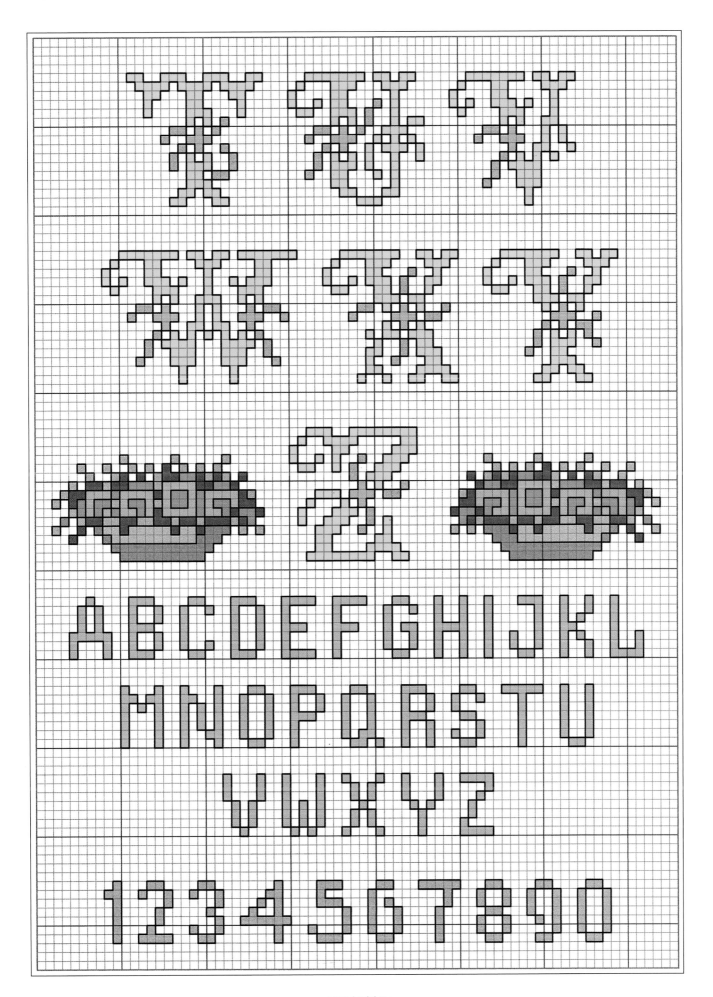

CHART 24

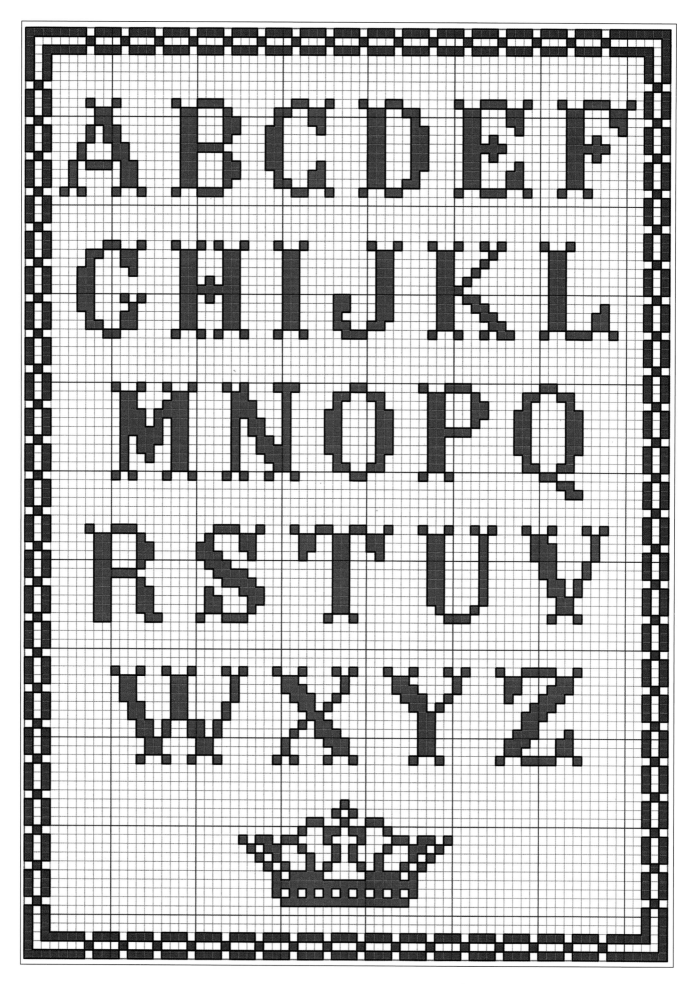

CHART 25

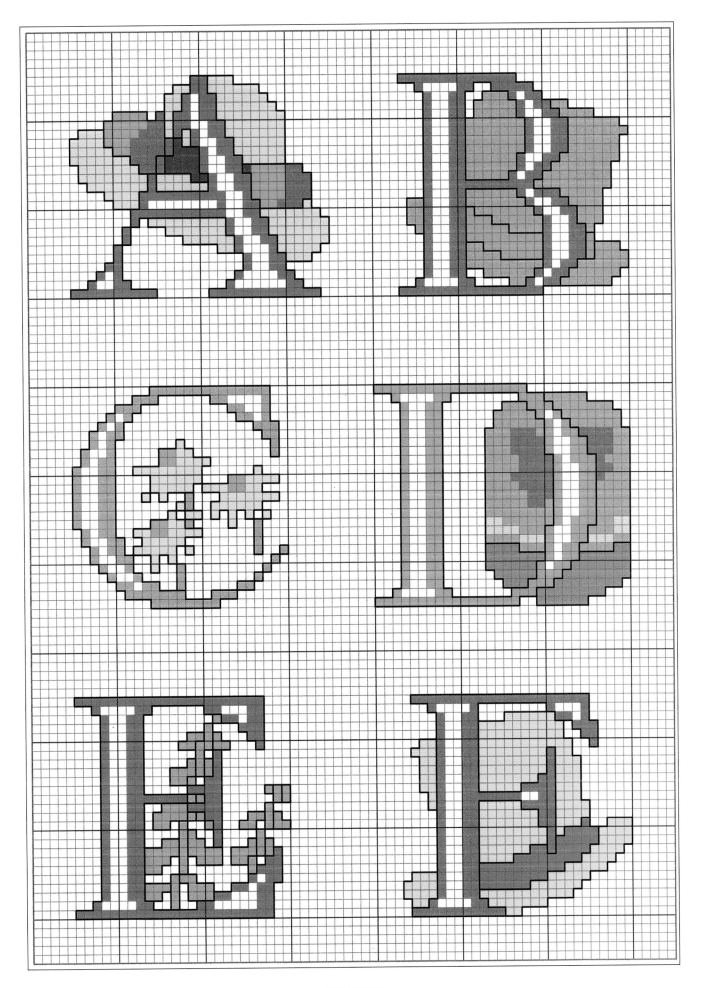

CHART 26

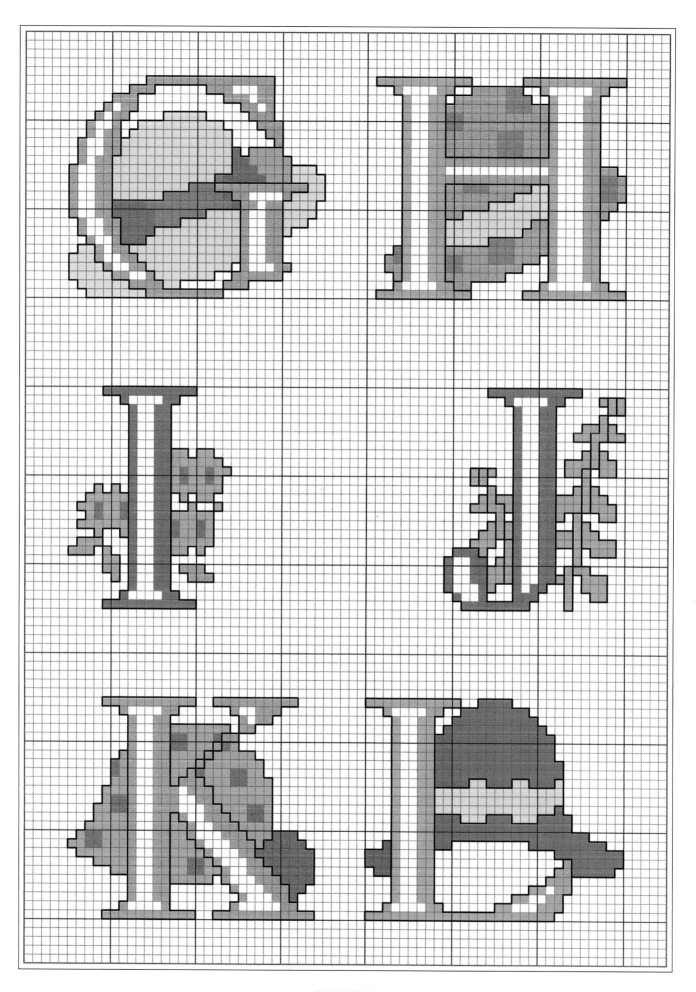

CHART 27

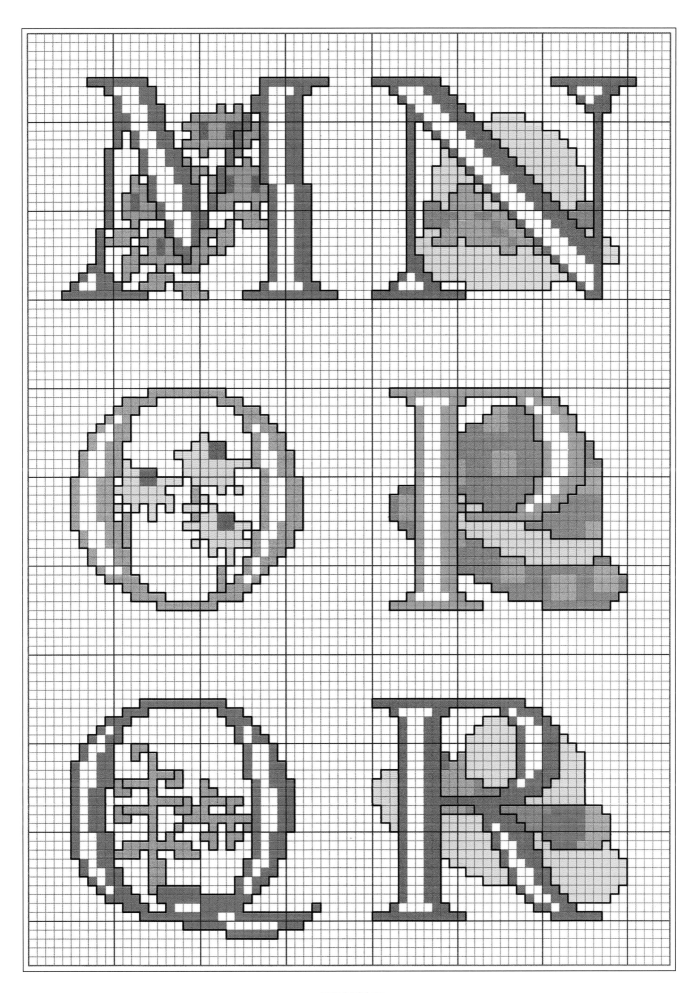

CHART 28

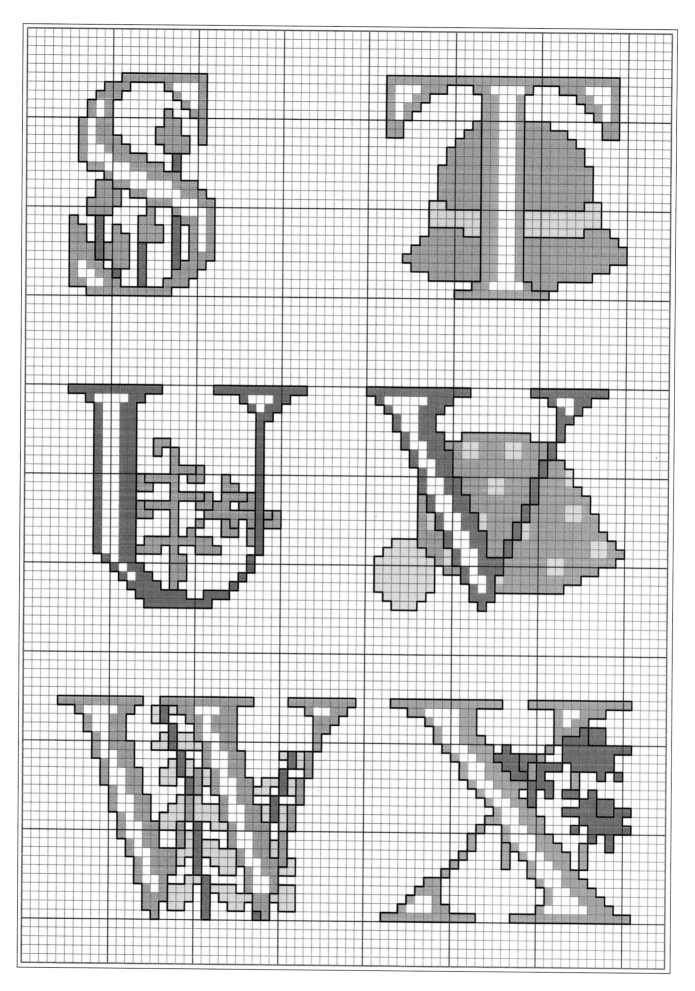

CHART 29

CHART 30

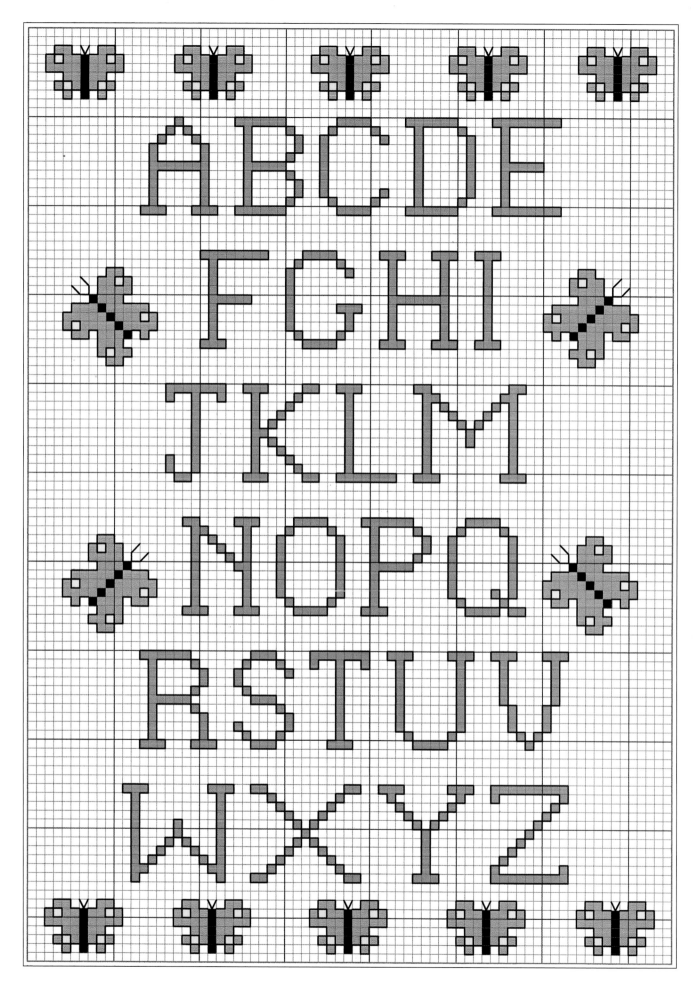

CHART 31

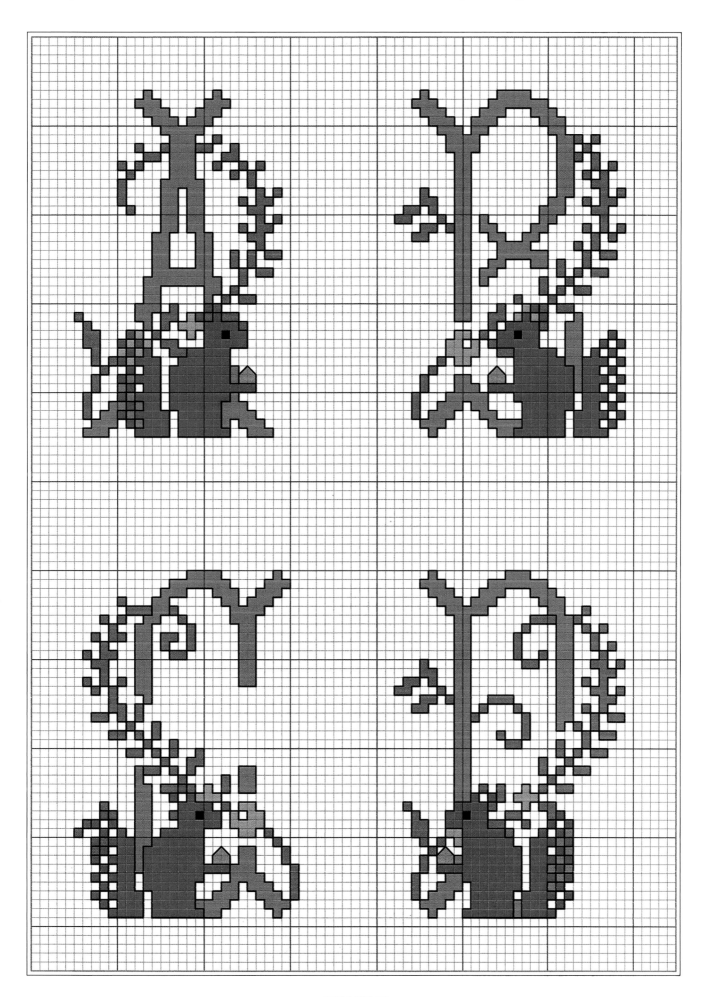

CHART 32

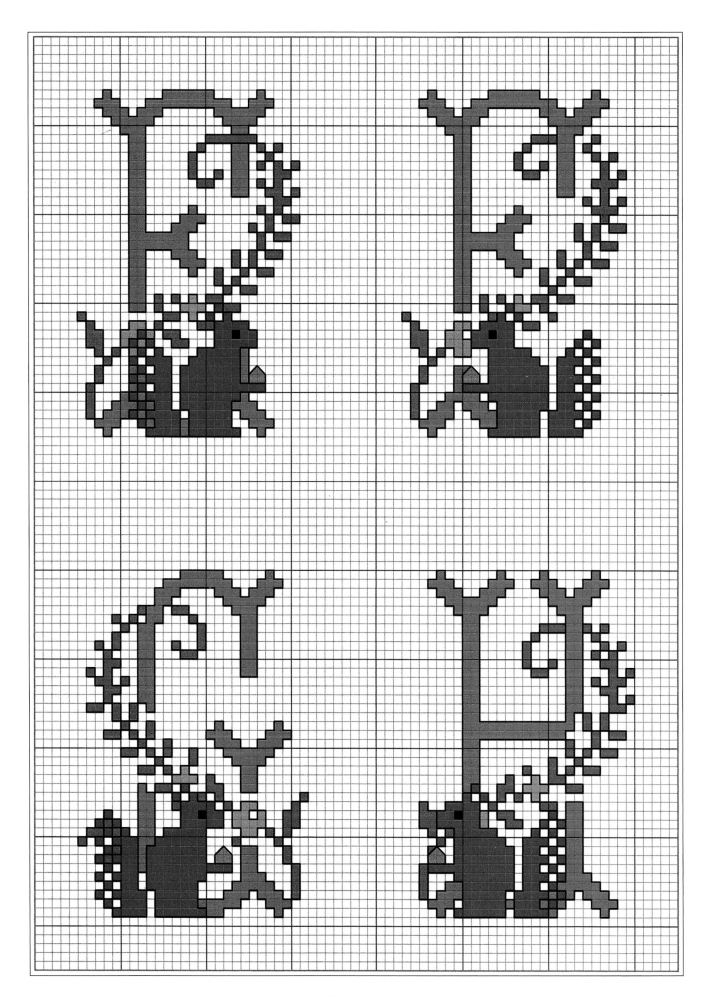

CHART 33

CHART 34

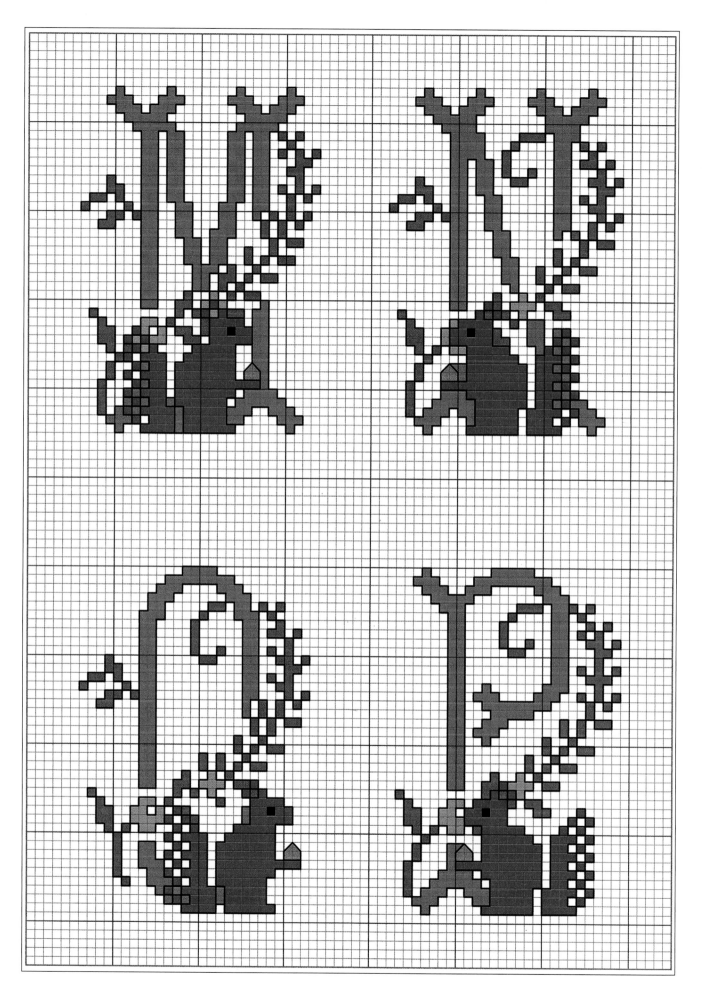

CHART 35

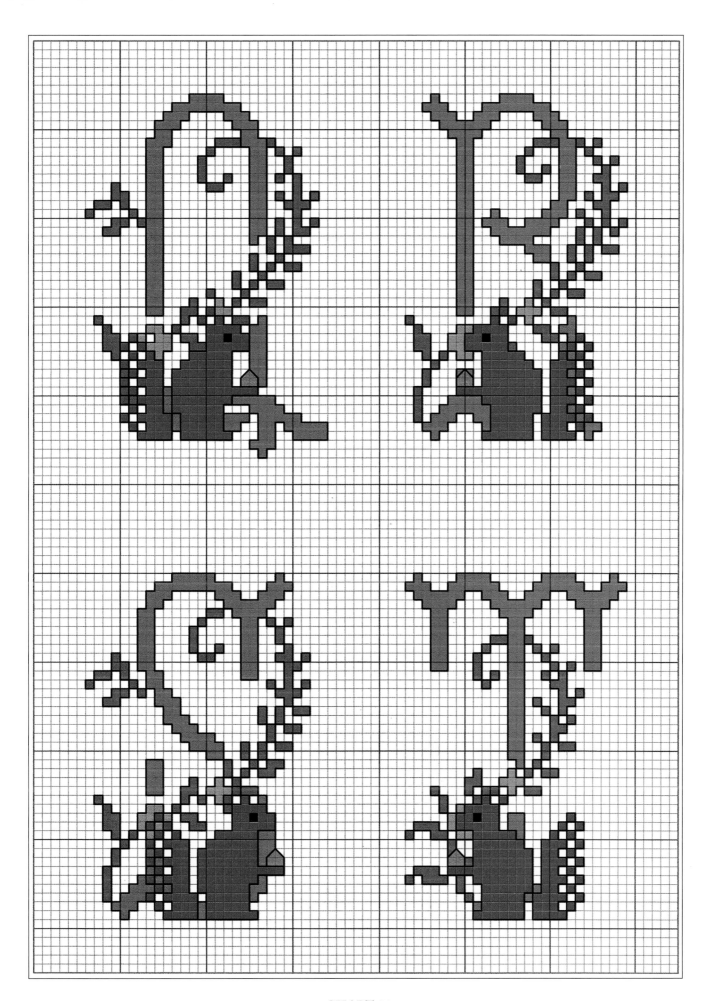

CHART 36

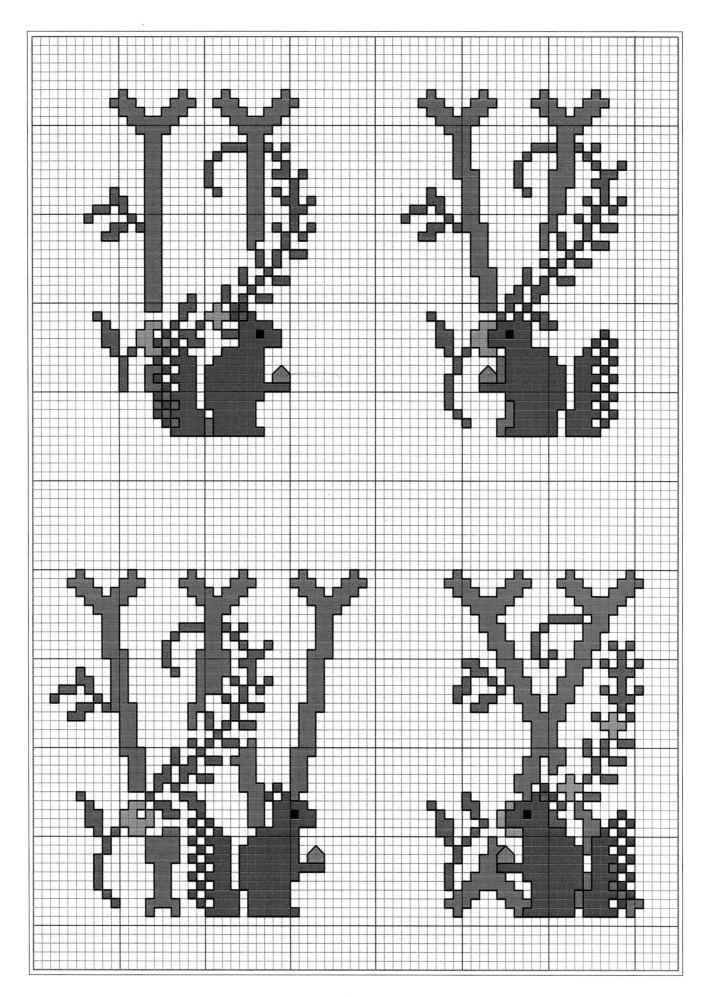

CHART 37

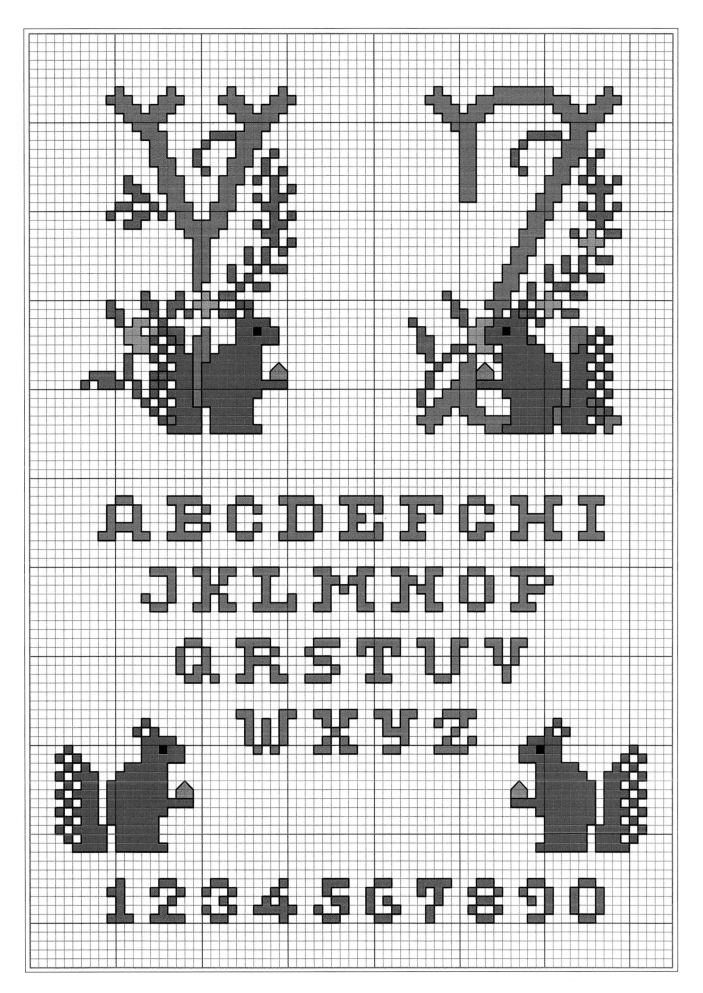

CHART 38

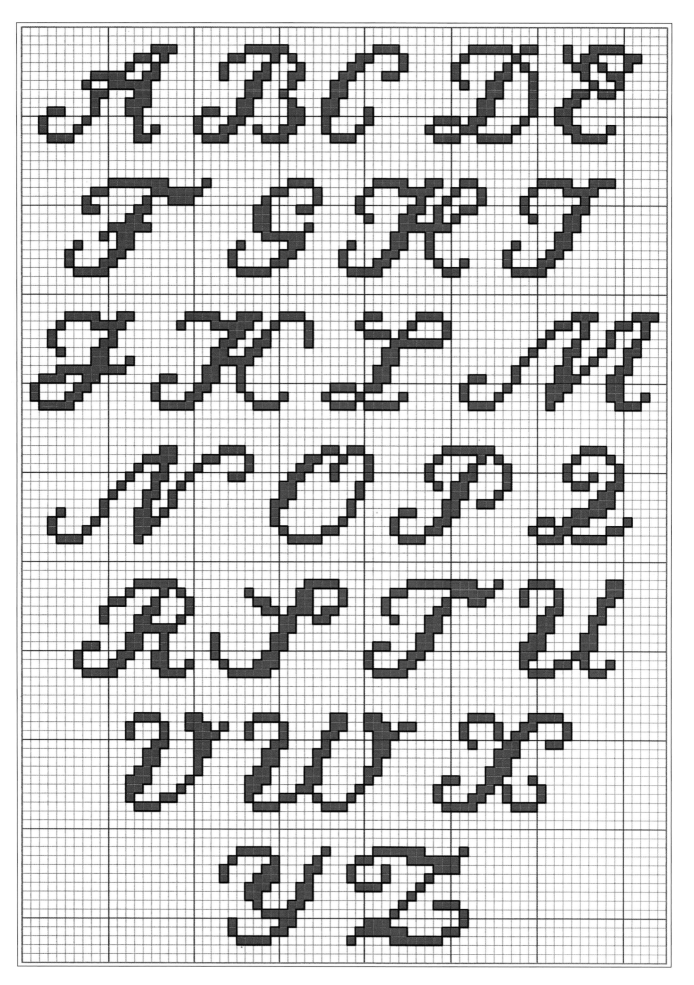

CHART 39

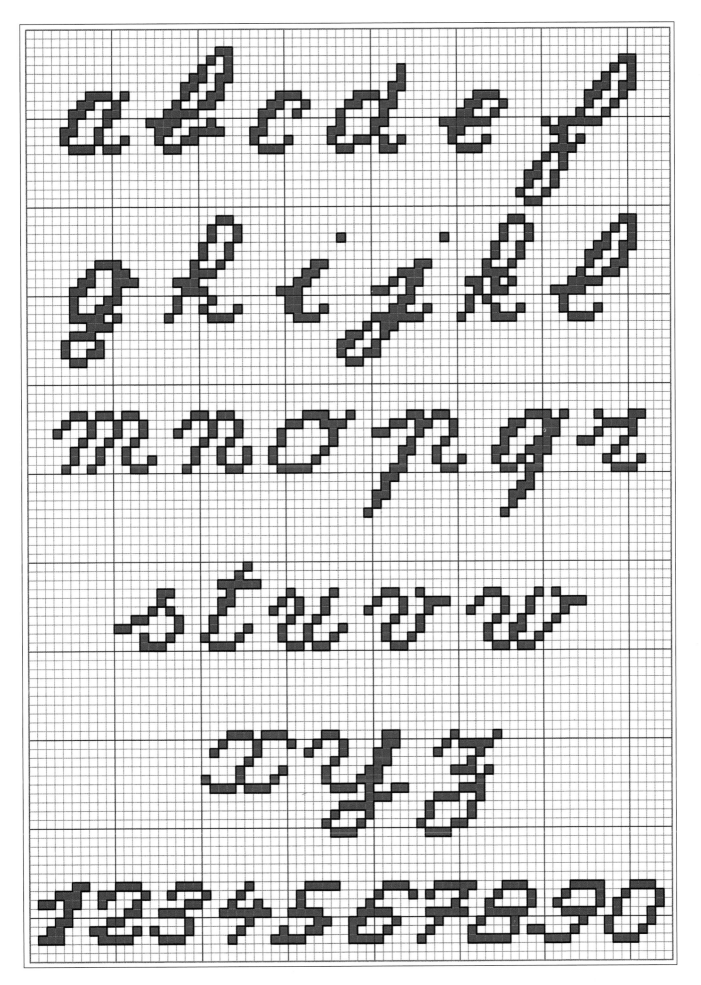

CHART 40

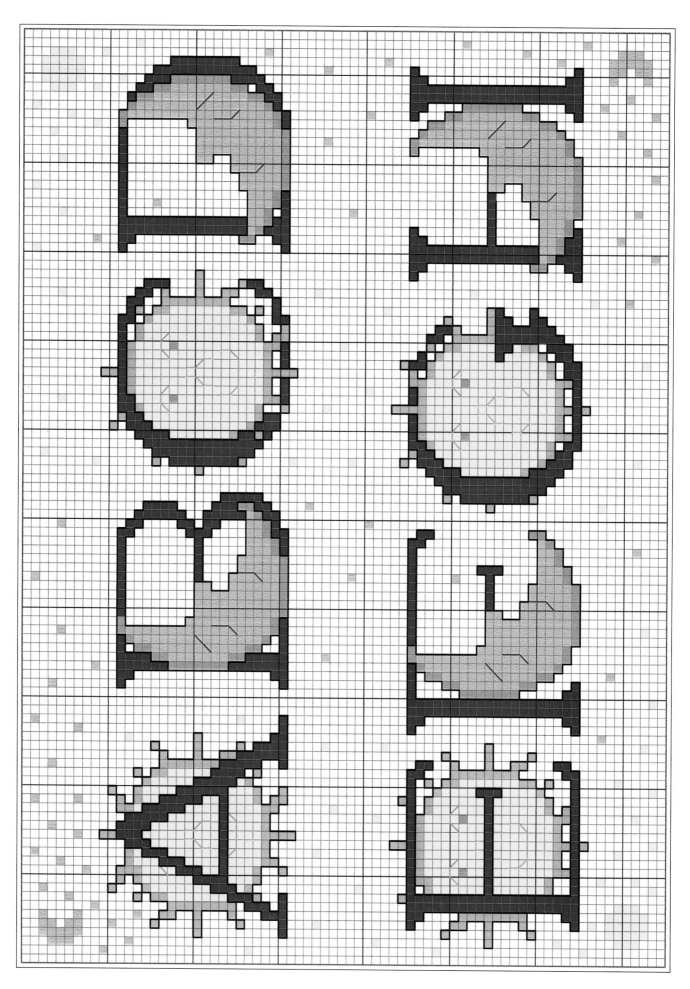

CHART 41

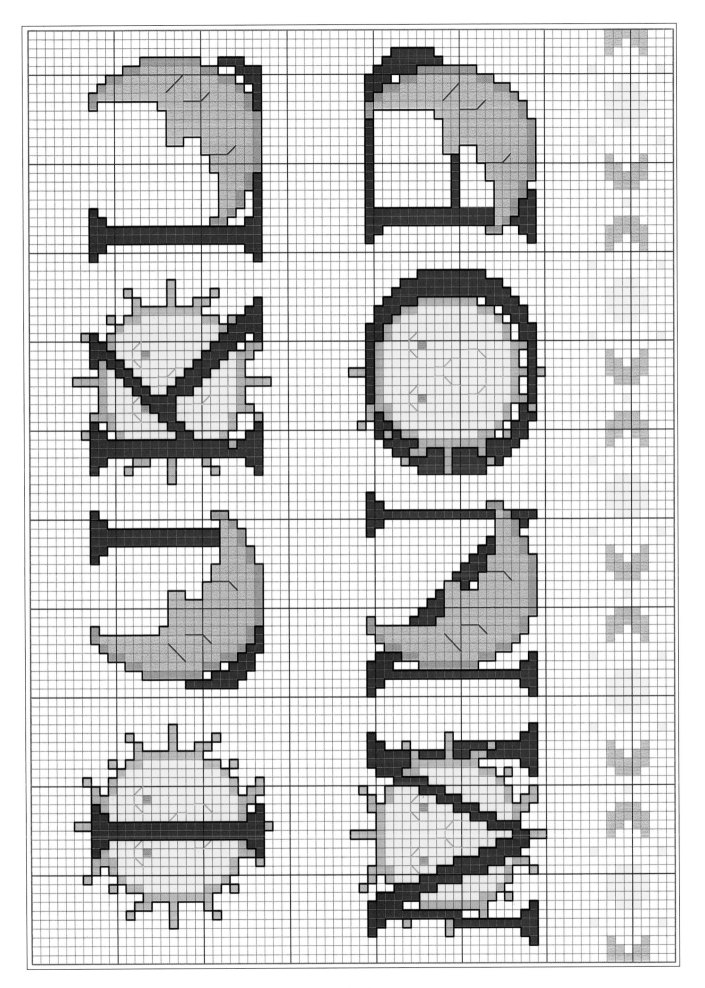

CHART 42

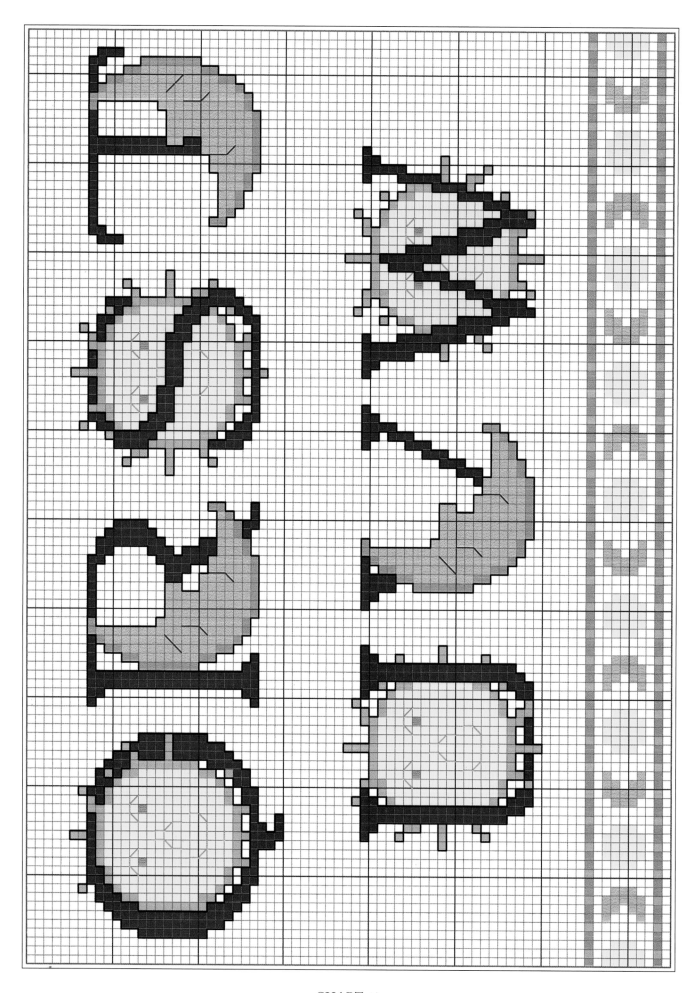

CHART 43

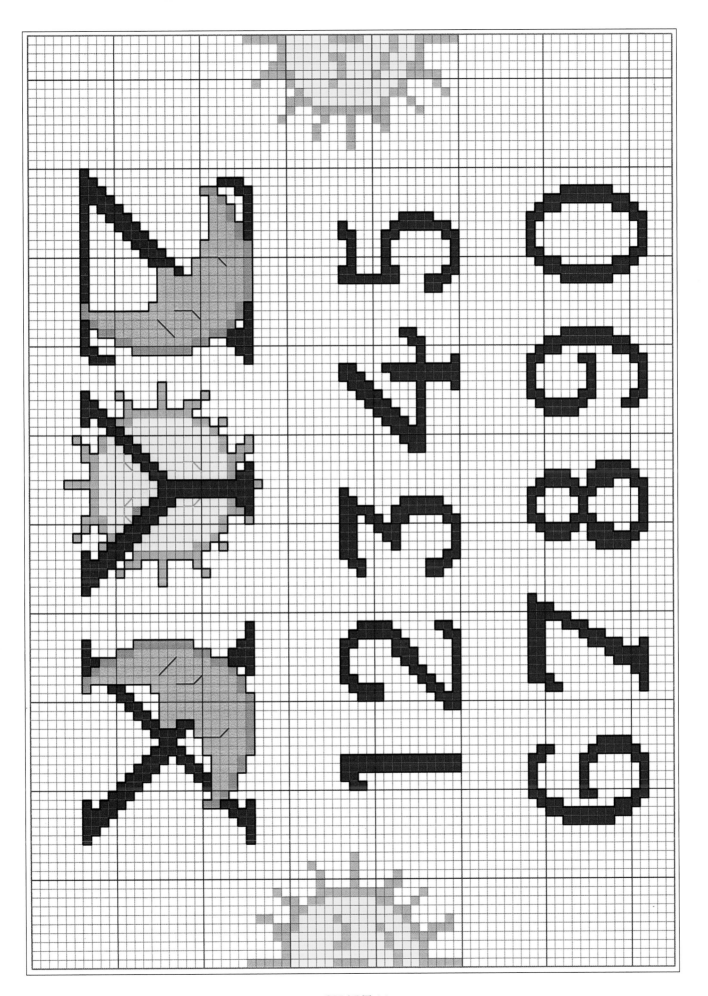

CHART 44

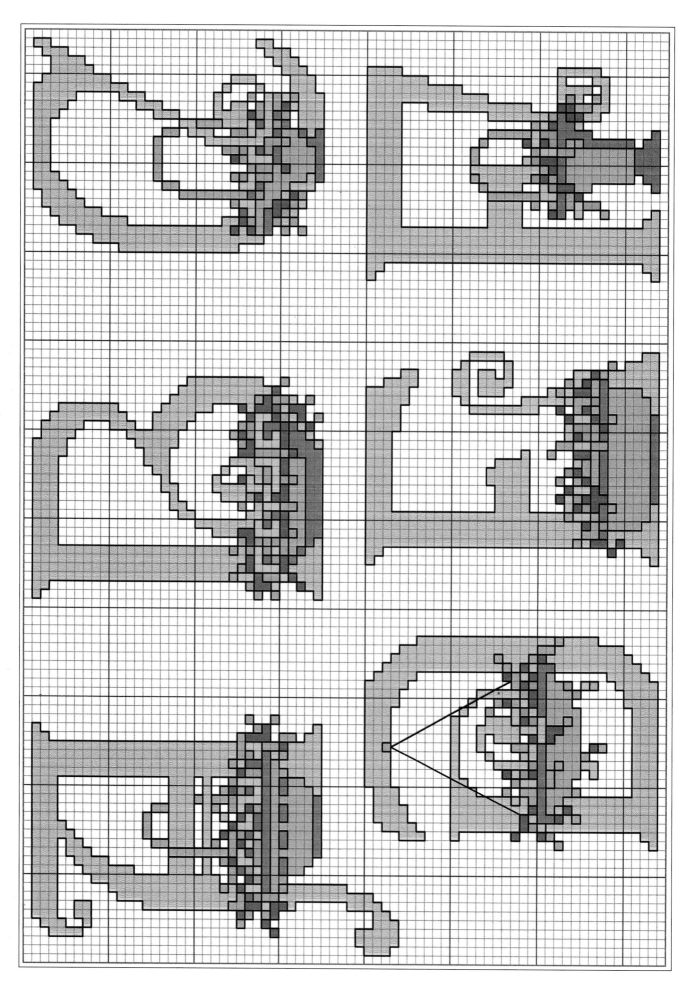

CHART 45

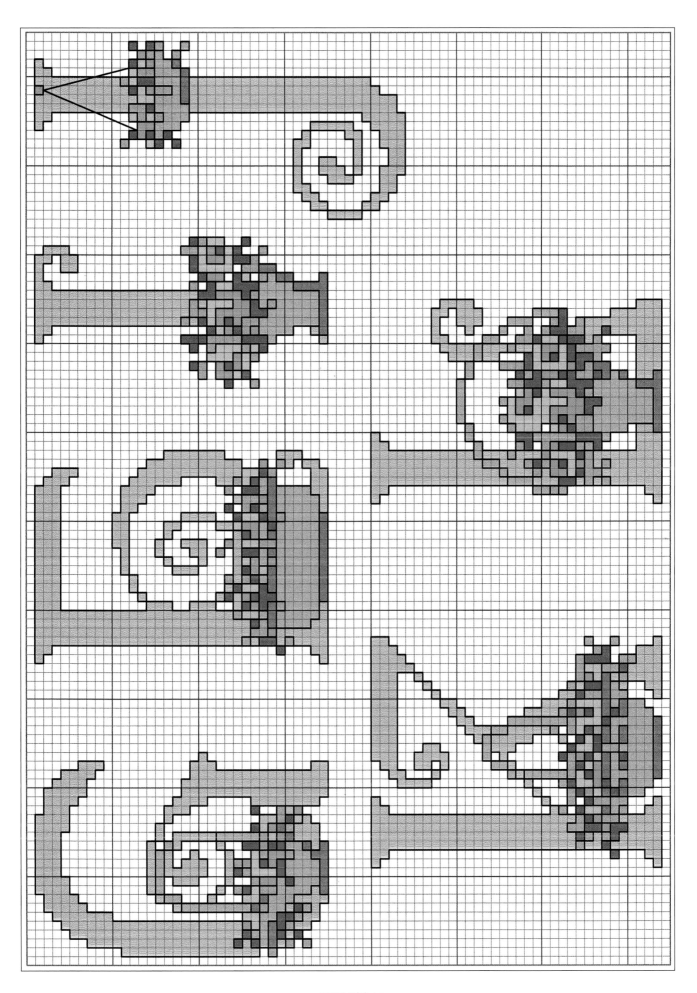

CHART 46

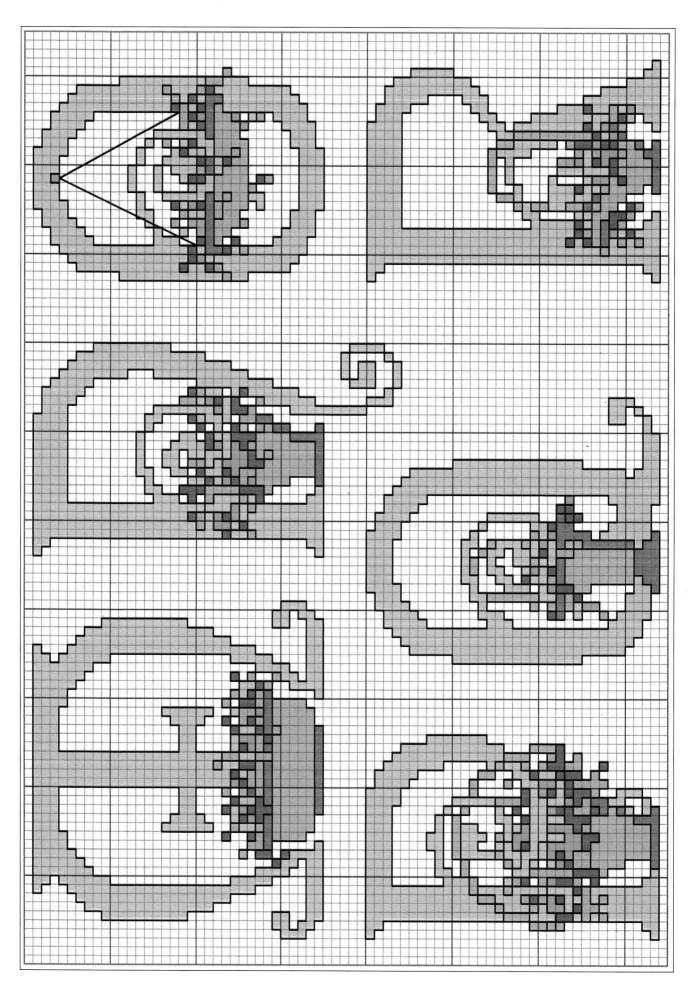

CHART 47

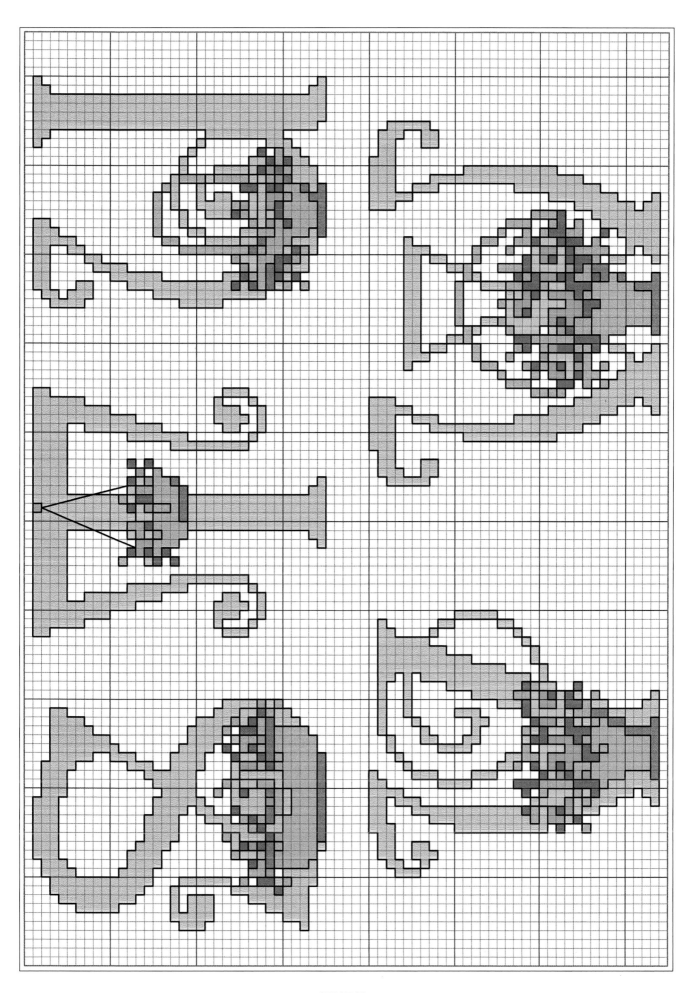

CHART 48

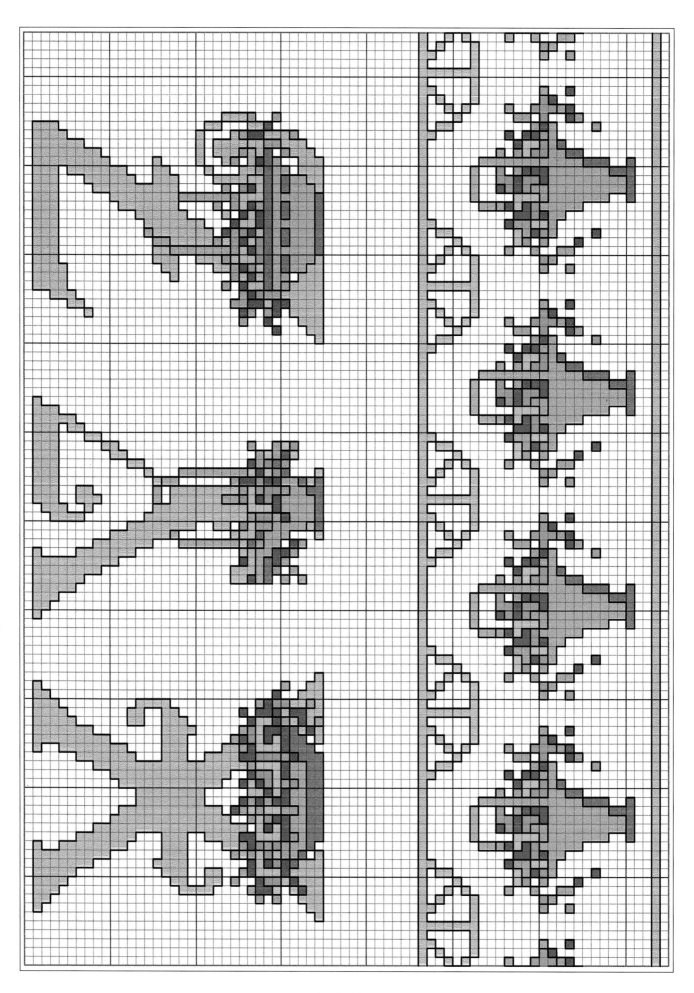

CHART 49

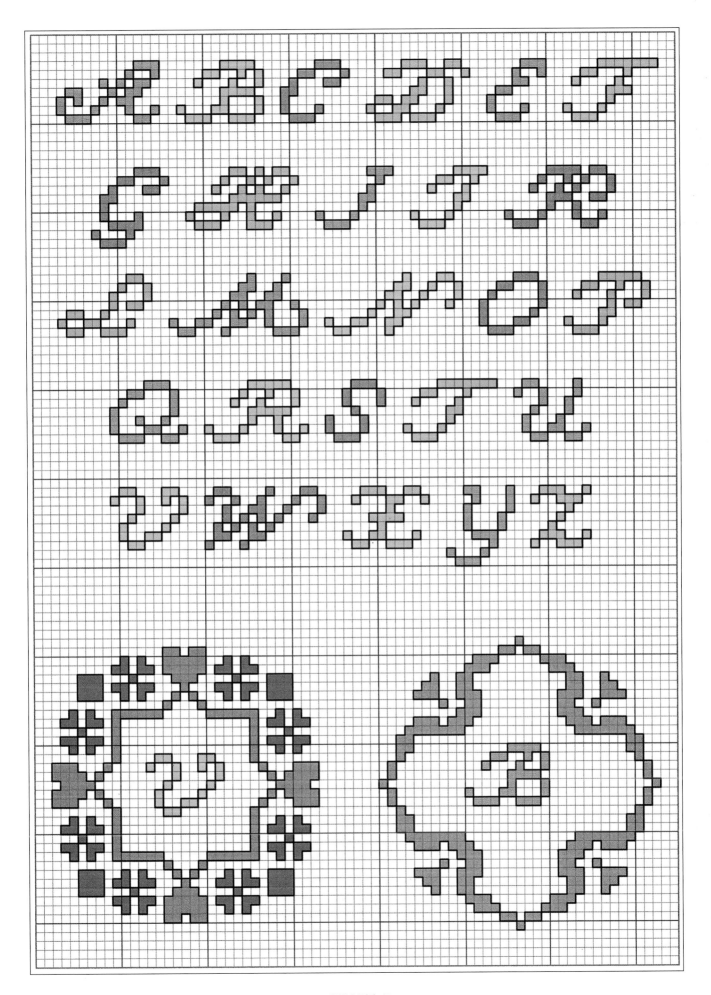

CHART 50

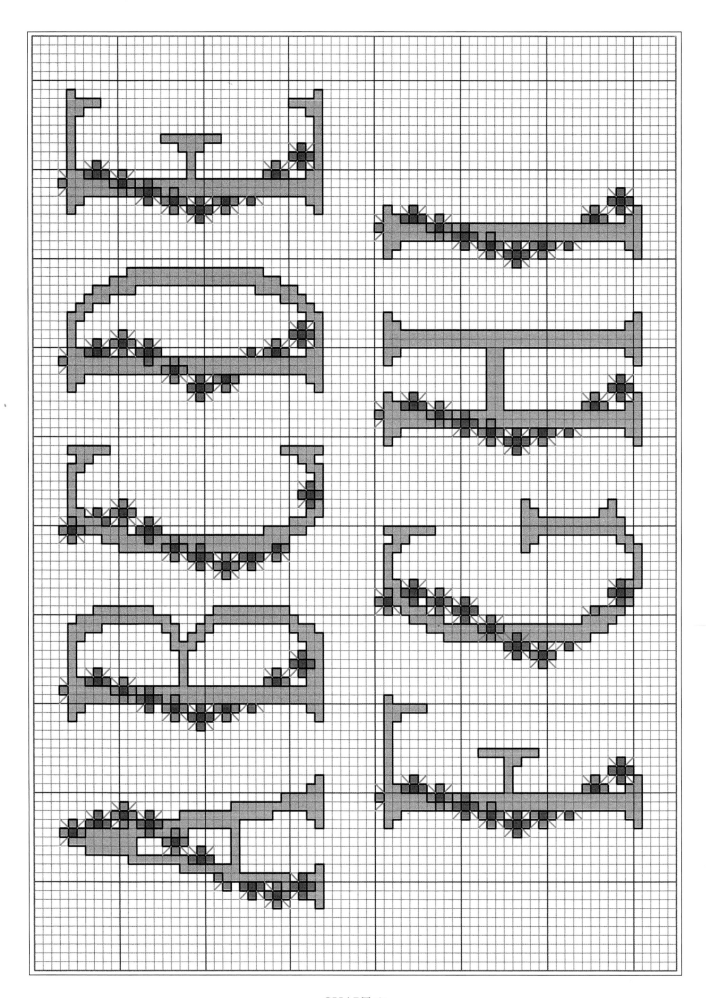

CHART 51

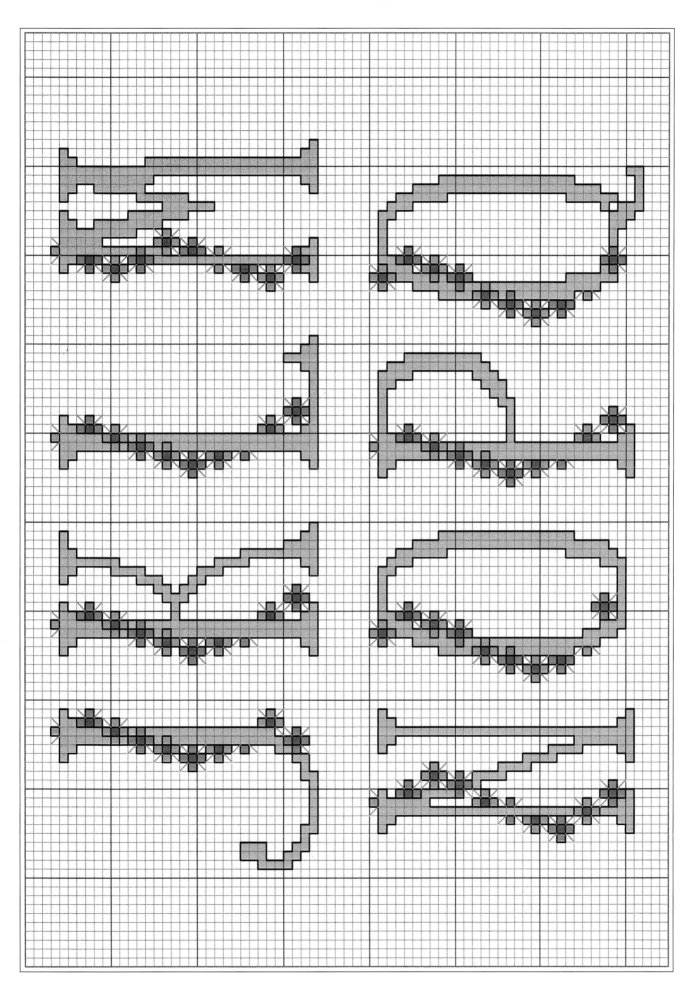

CHART 52

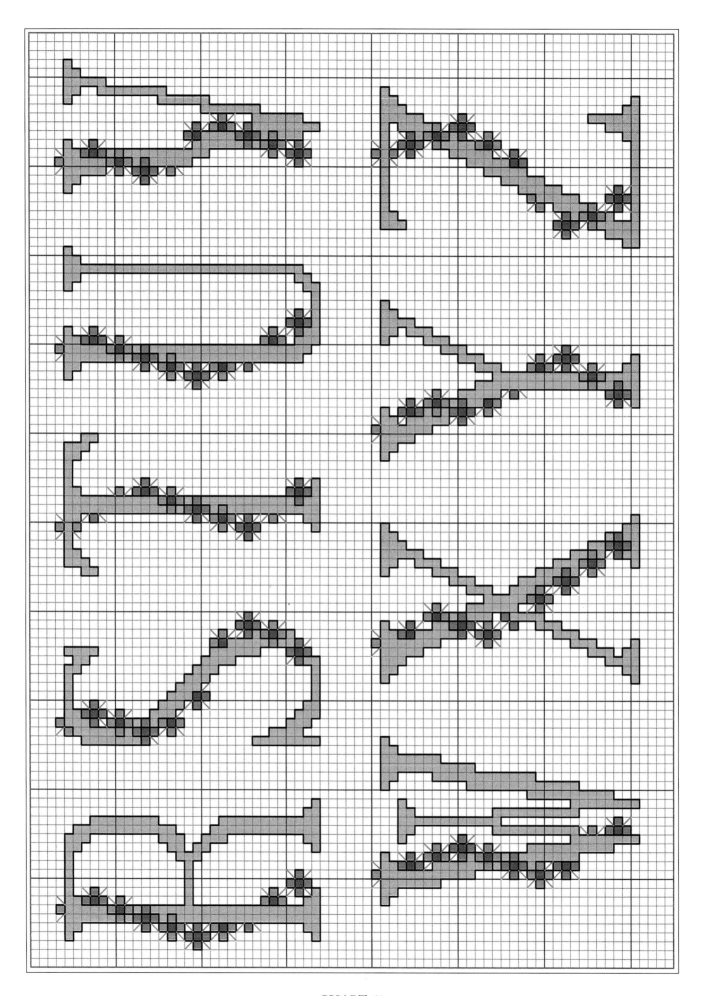

CHART 53

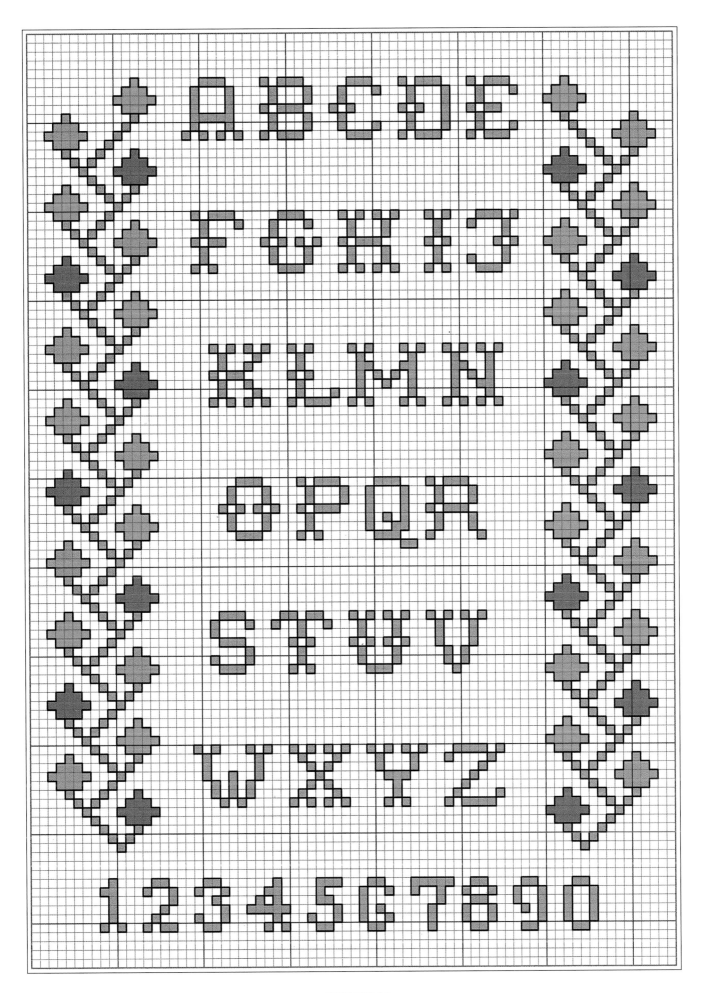

CHART 54

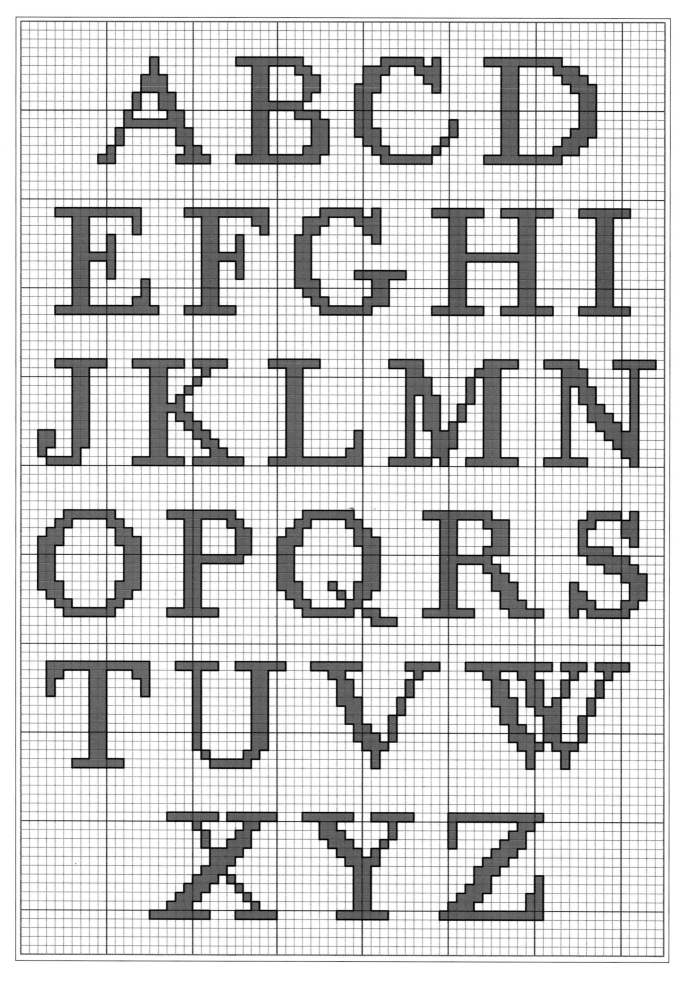

CHART 55

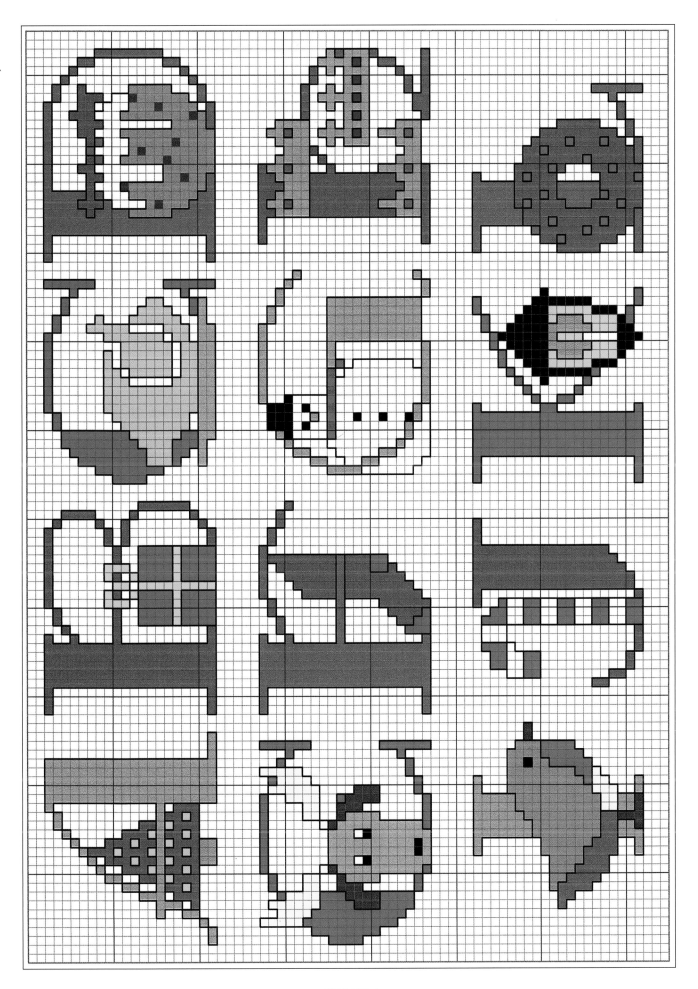

CHART 56

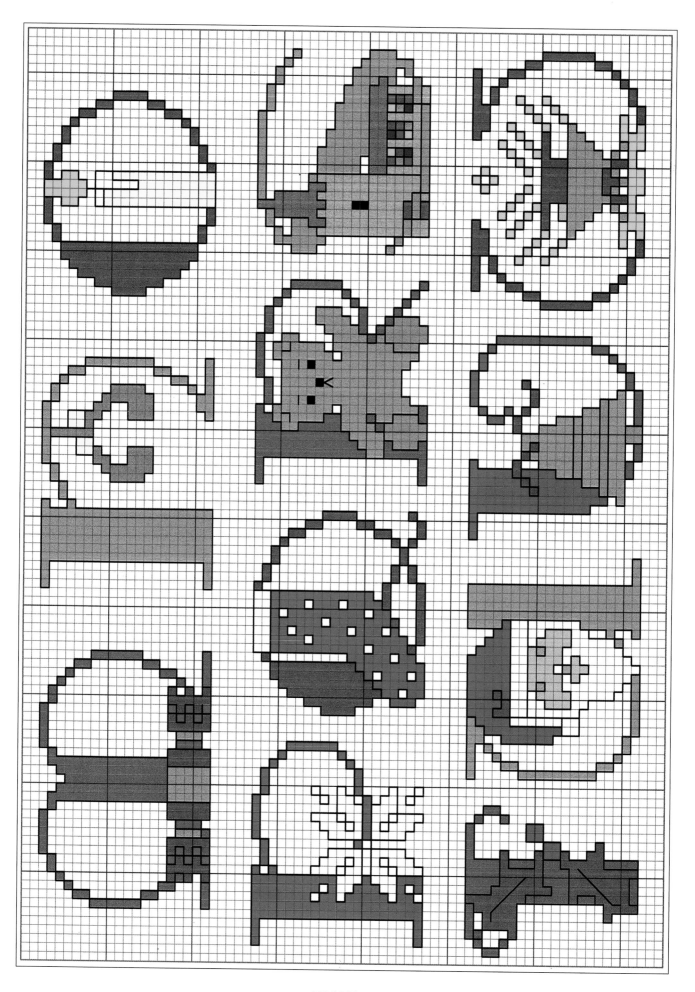

CHART 57

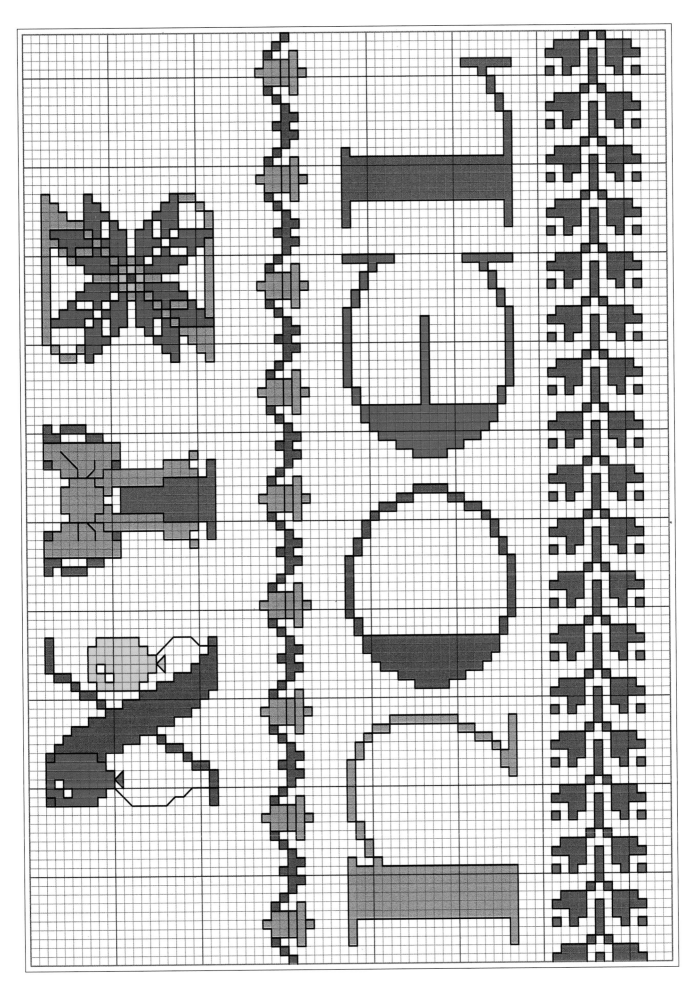

CHART 58

CHART 59

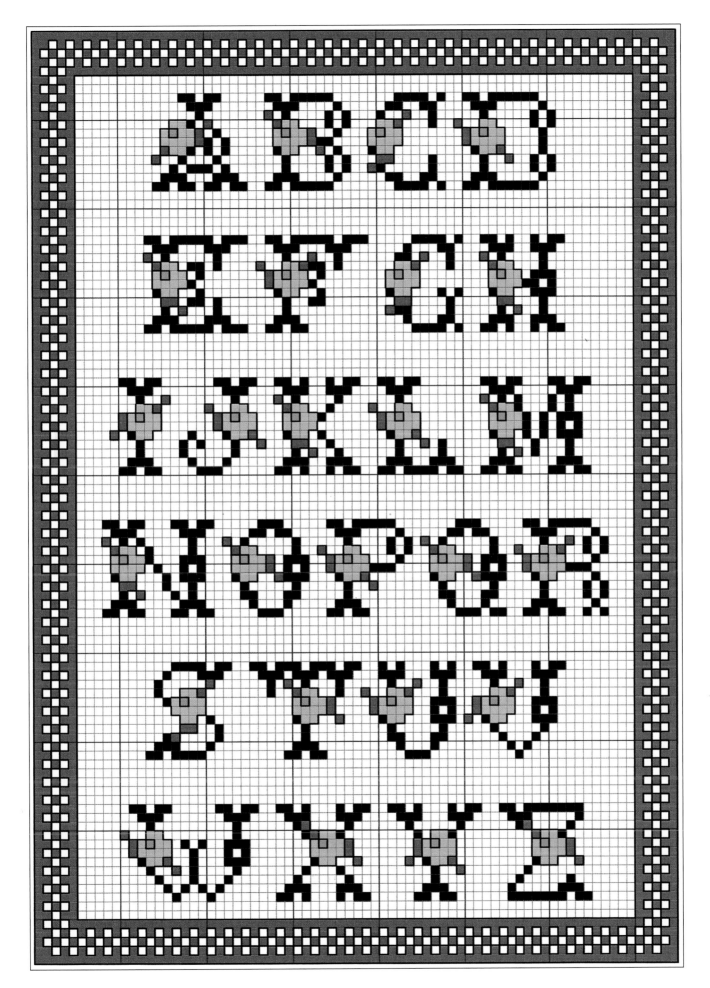

CHART 60

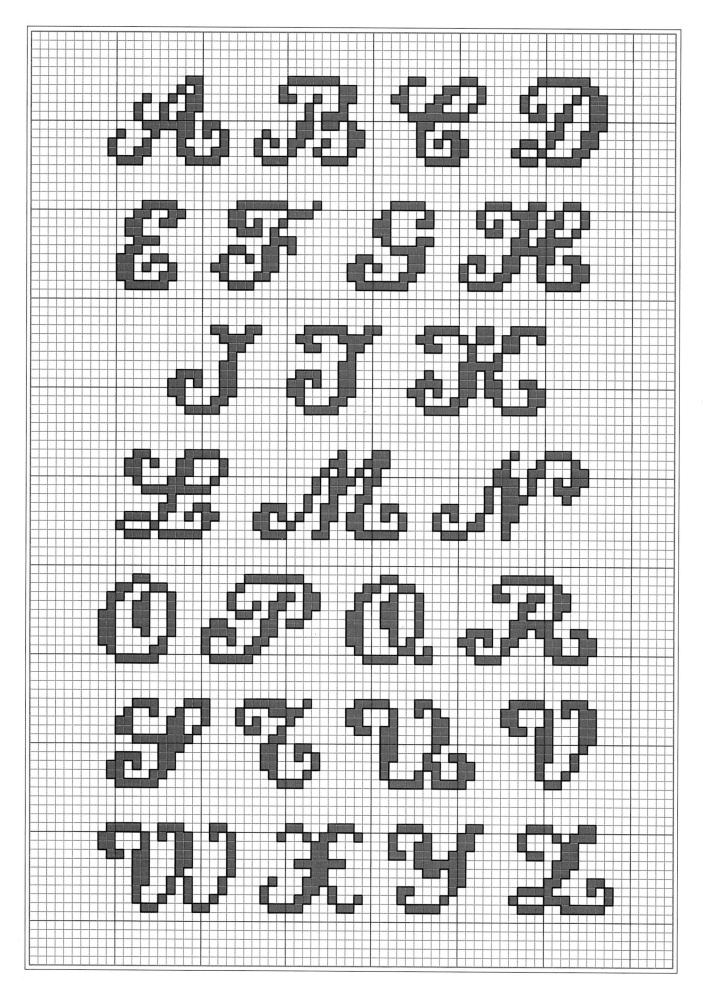

CHART 61

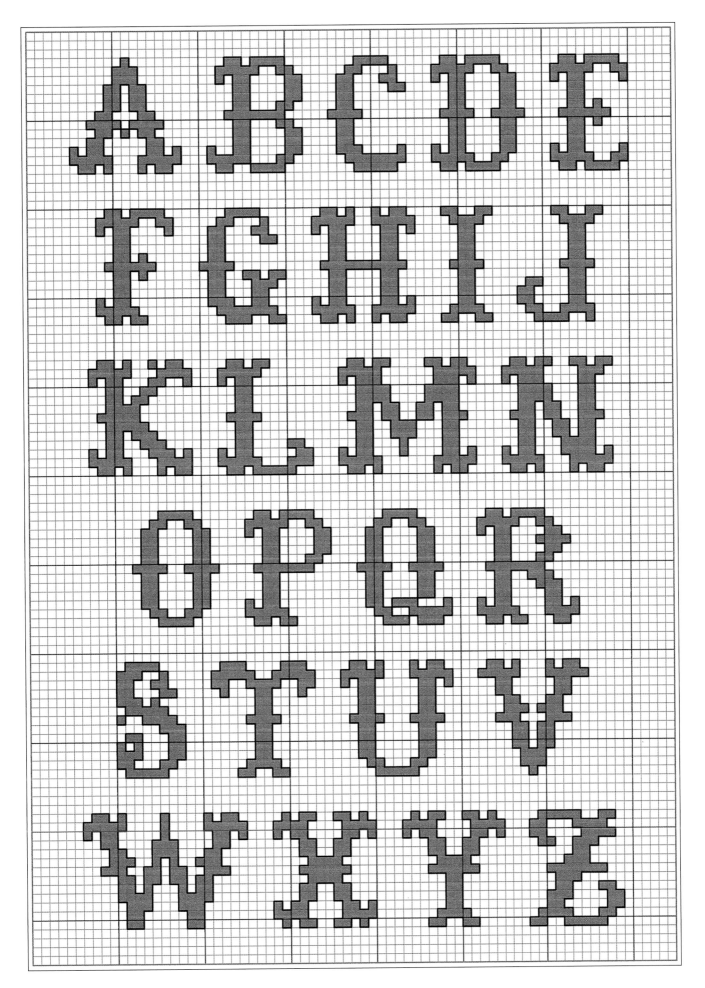

CHART 62

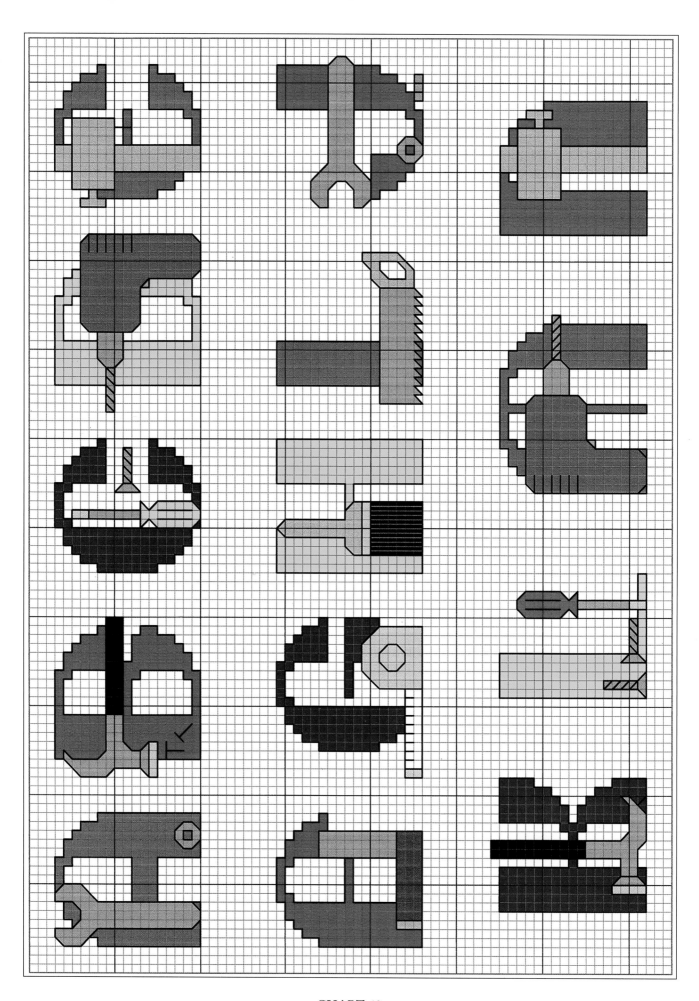

CHART 63

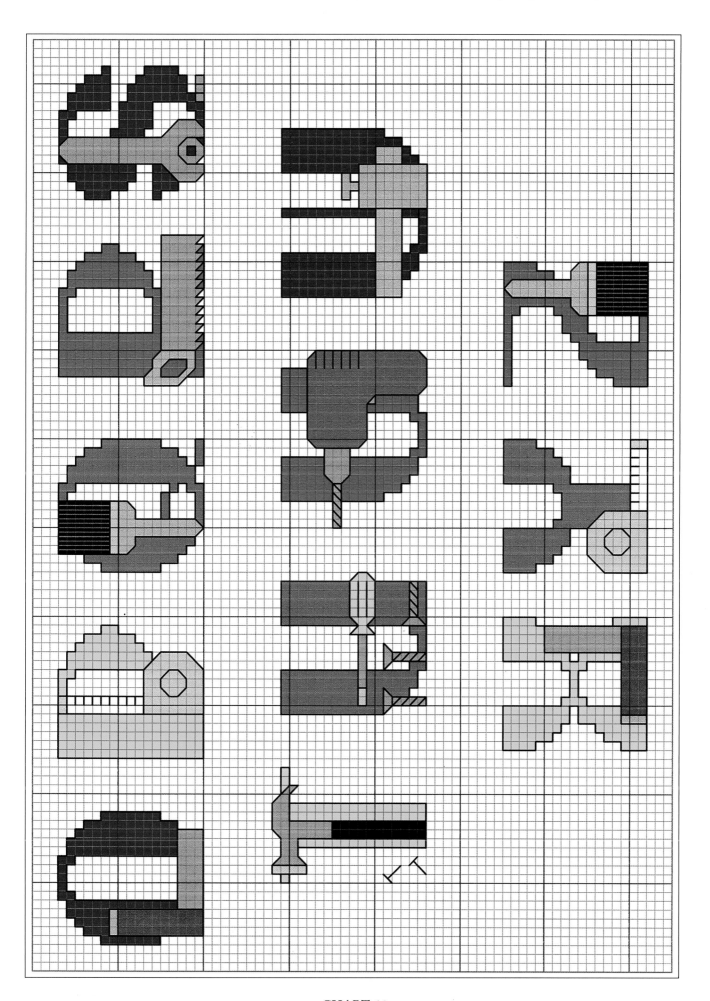

CHART 64

CHART 65

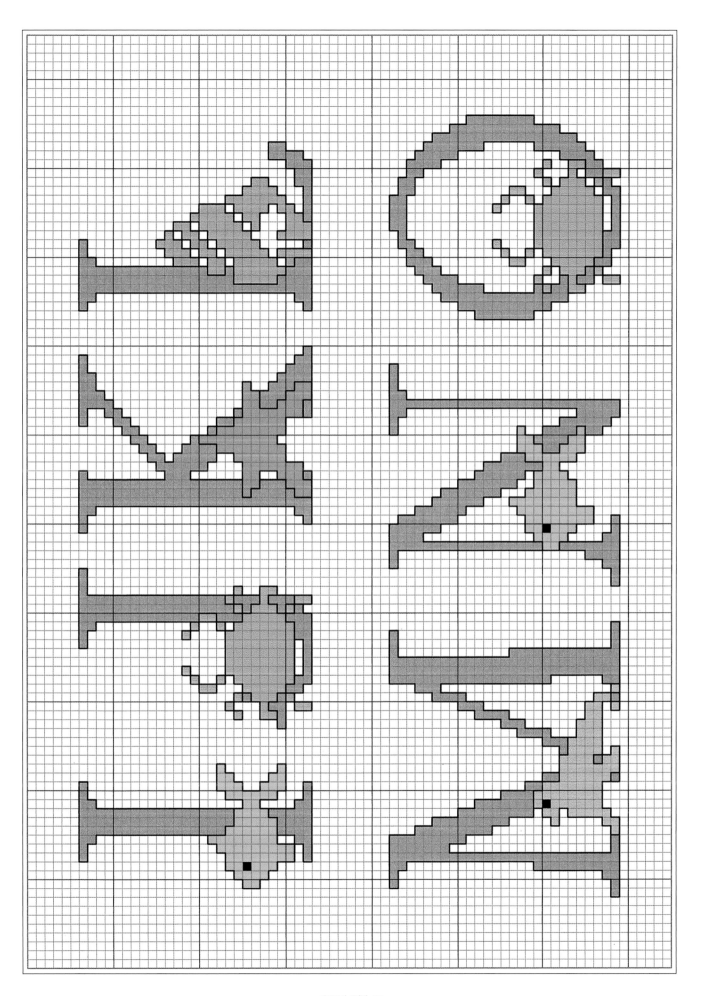

CHART 66

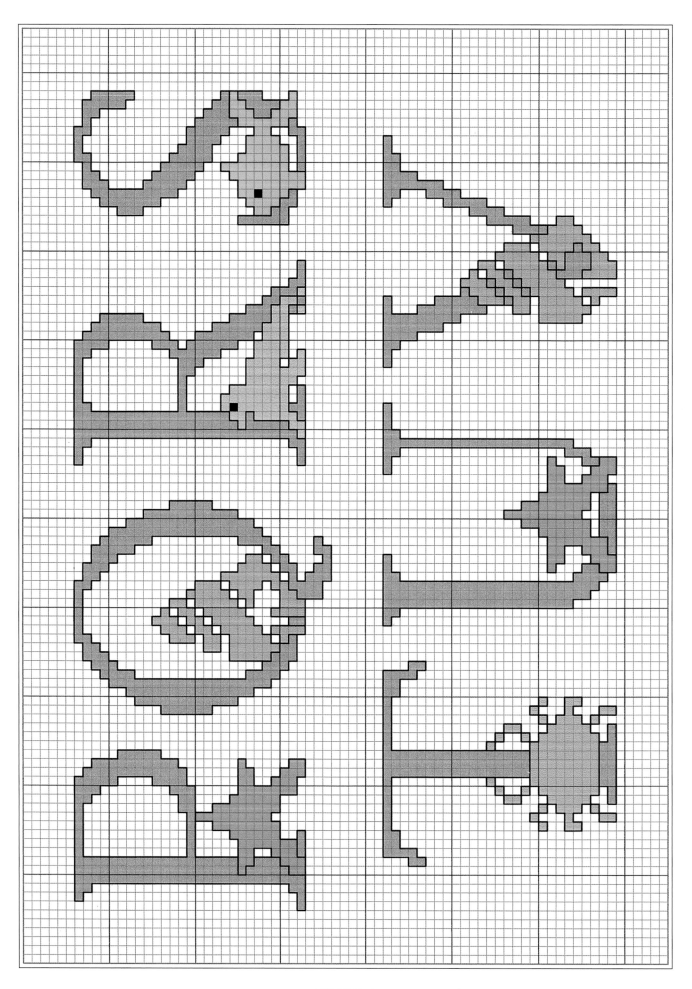

CHART 67

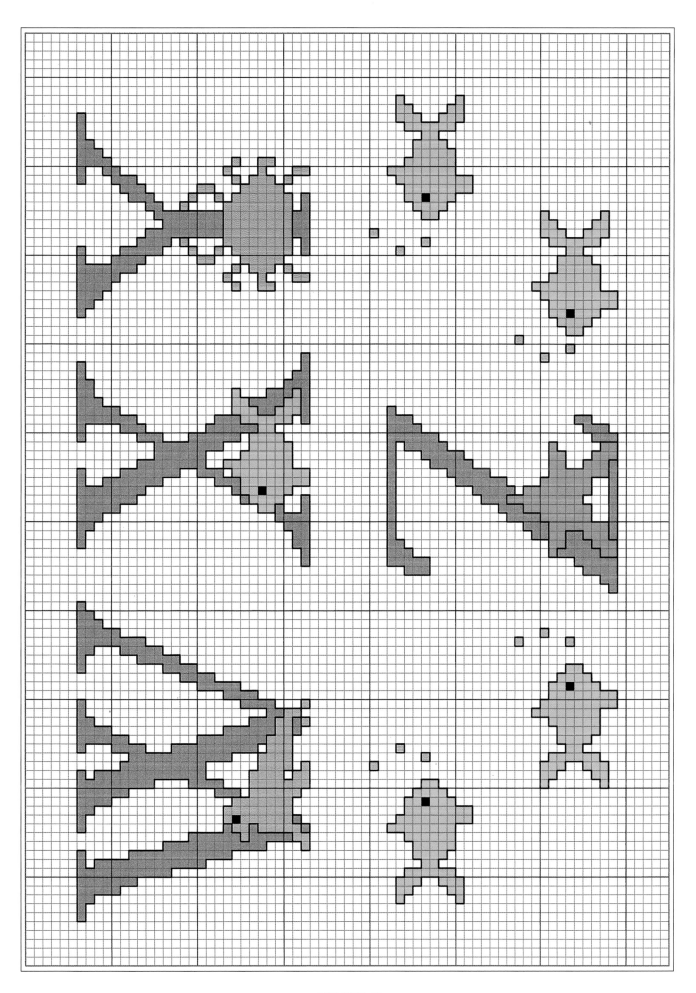

CHART 68

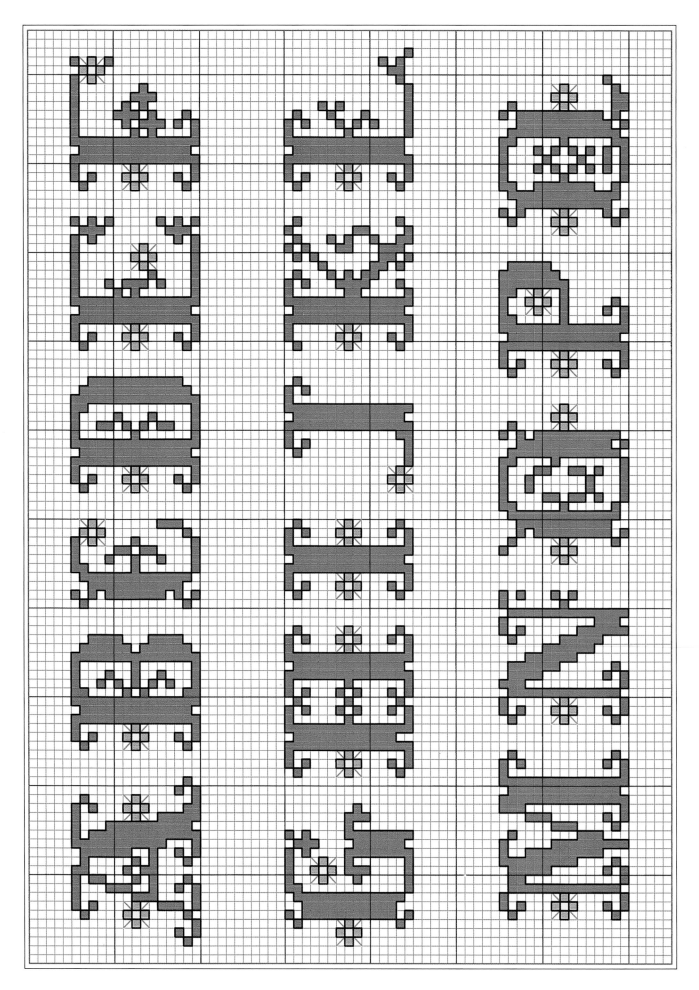

CHART 69

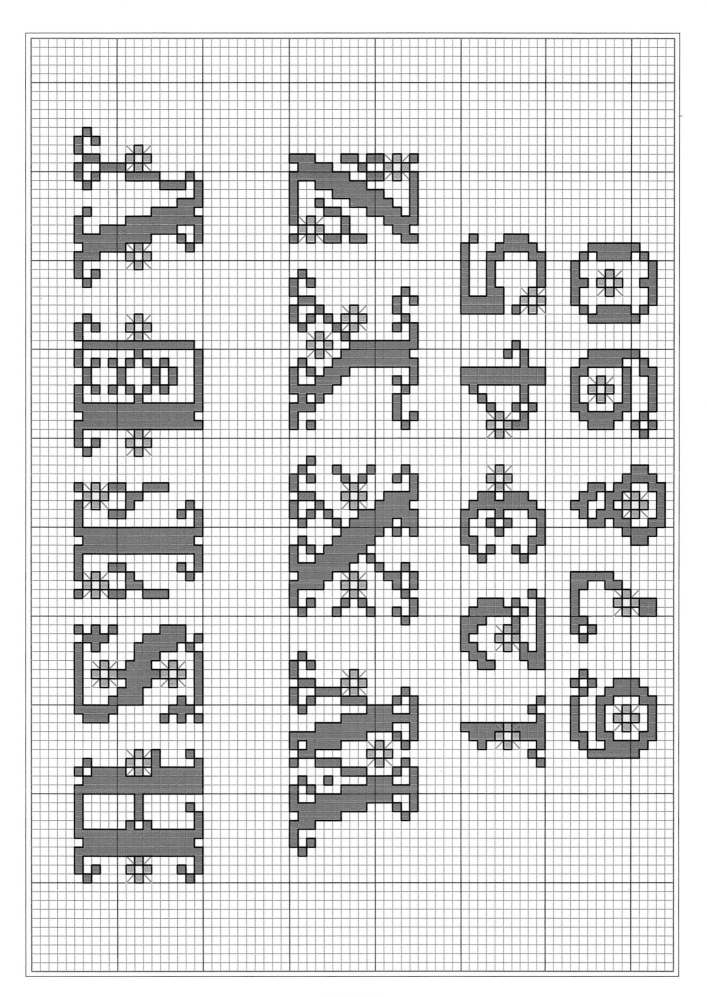

CHART 70

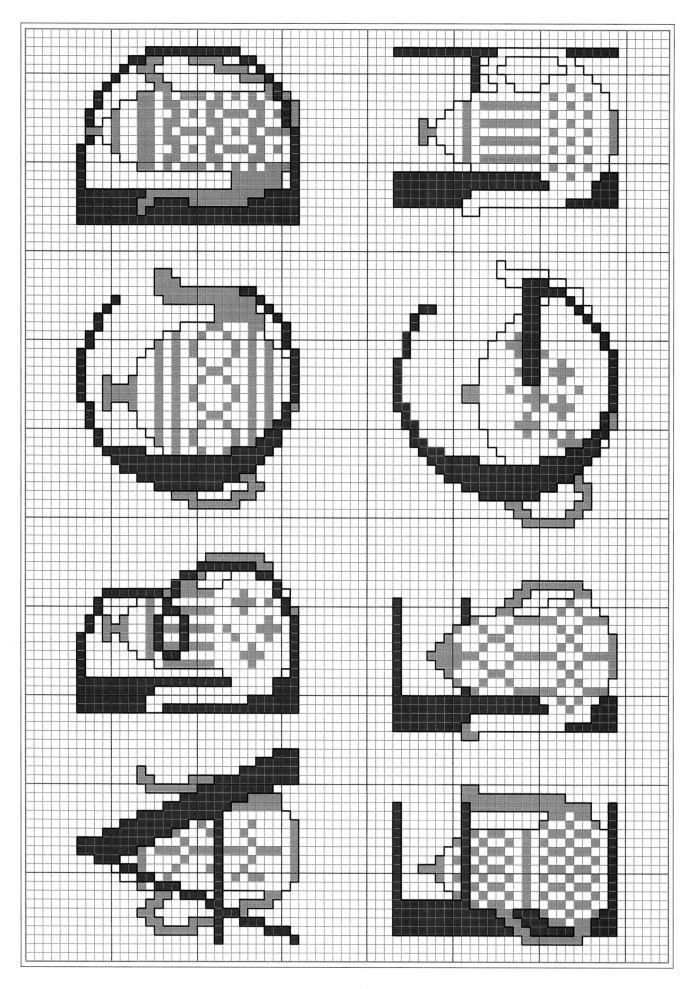

CHART 71

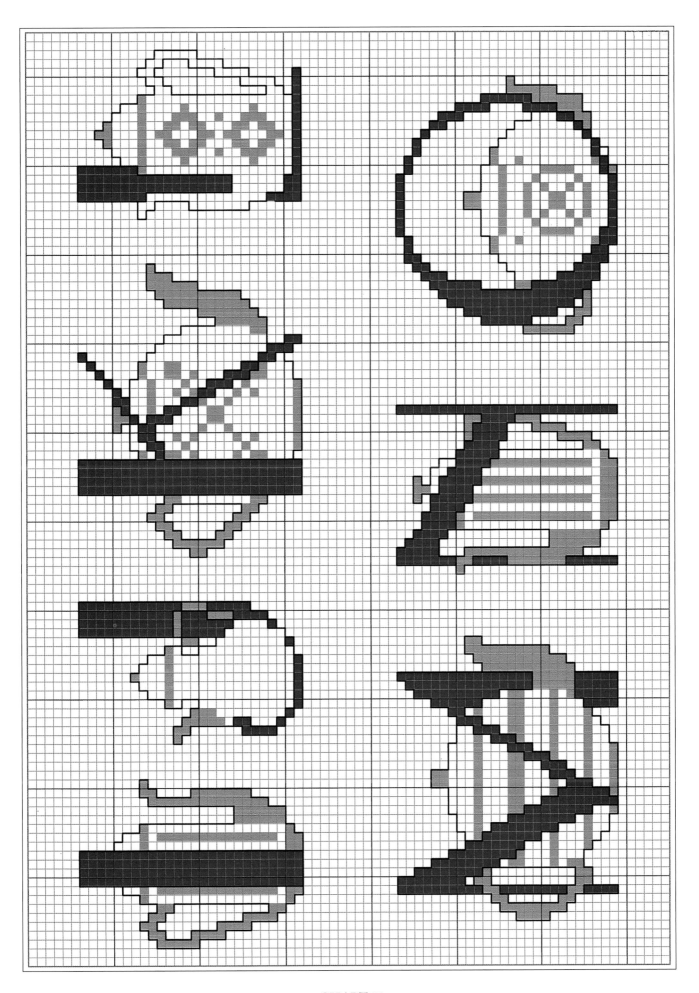

CHART 72

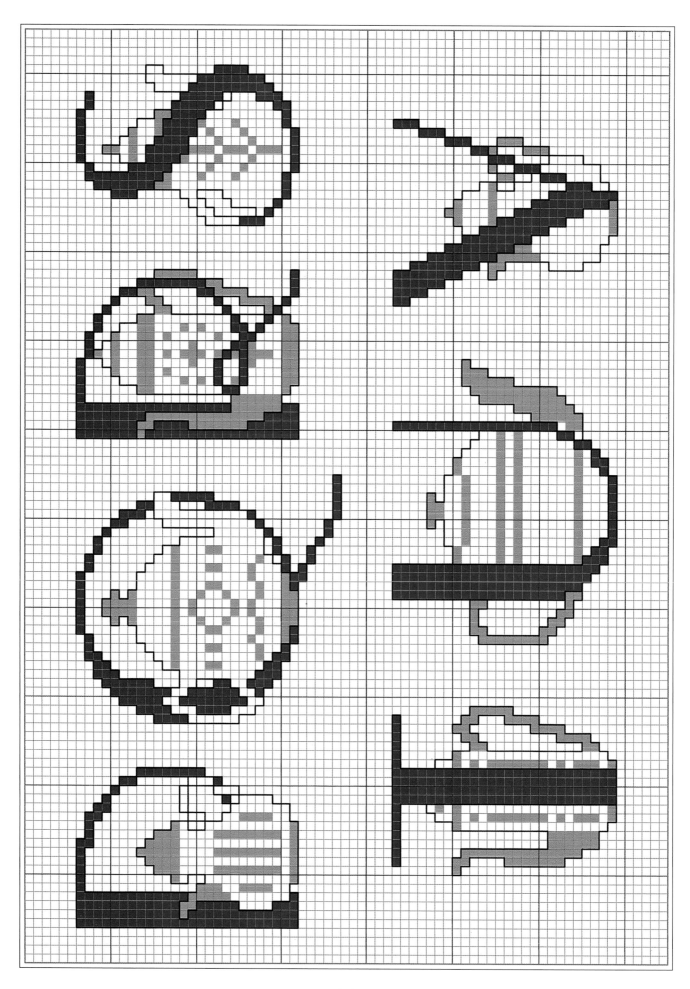

CHART 73

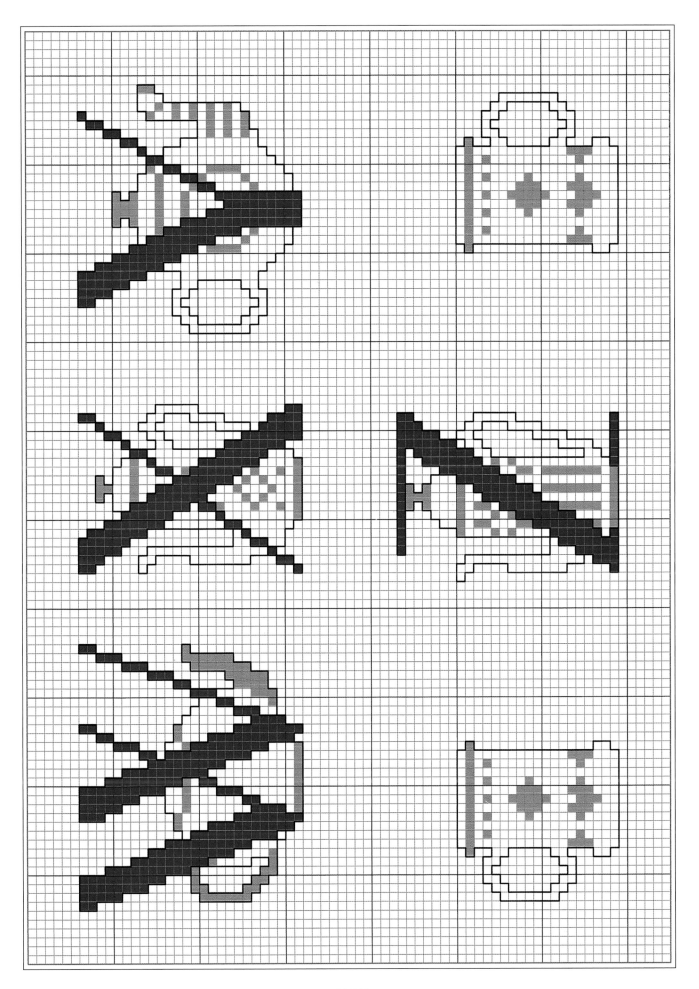

CHART 74

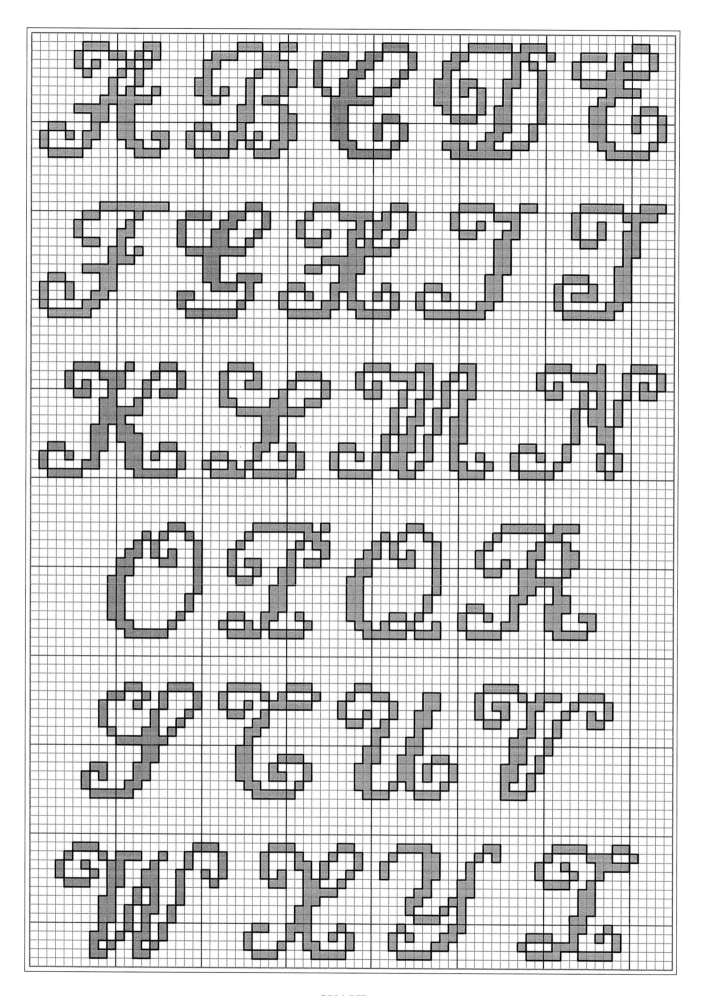

CHART 75

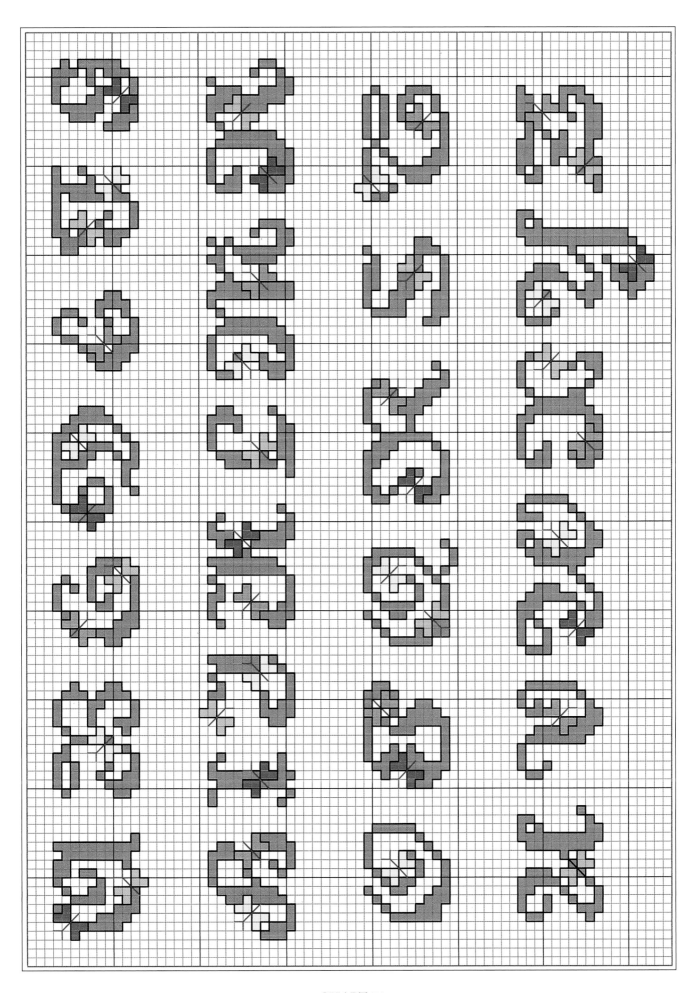

CHART 76

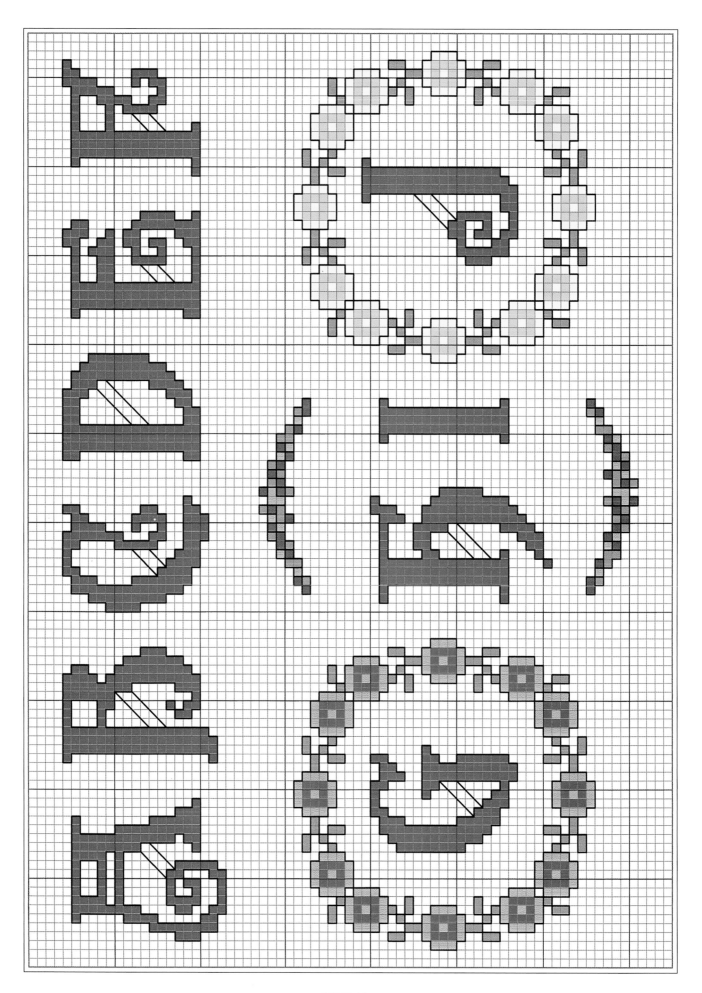

CHART 77

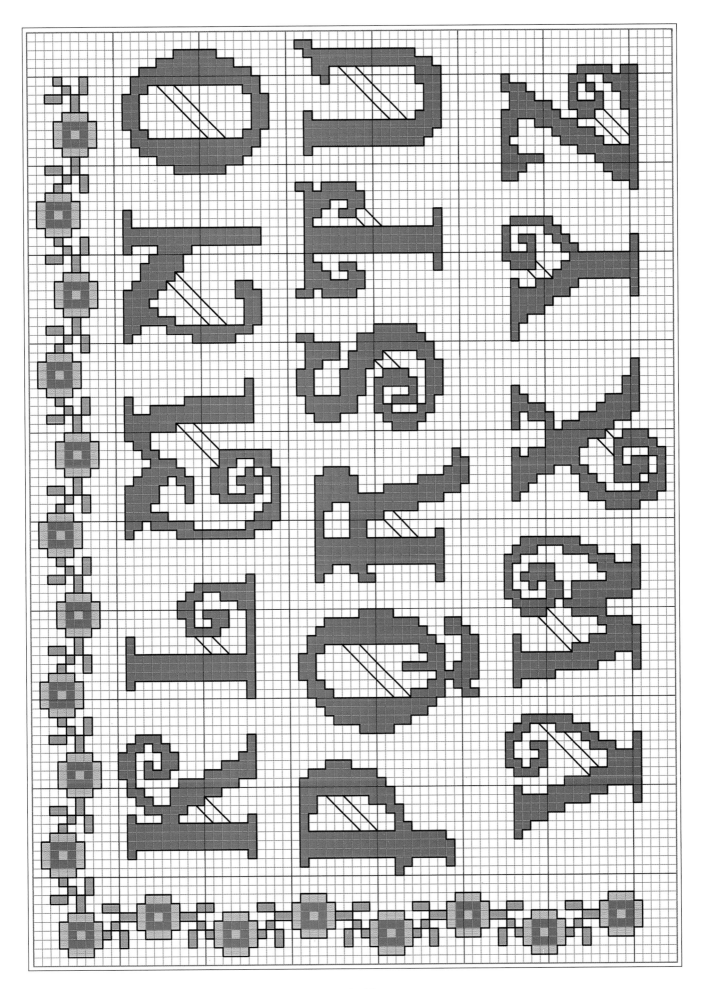

CHART 78

CHART 79

CHART 80

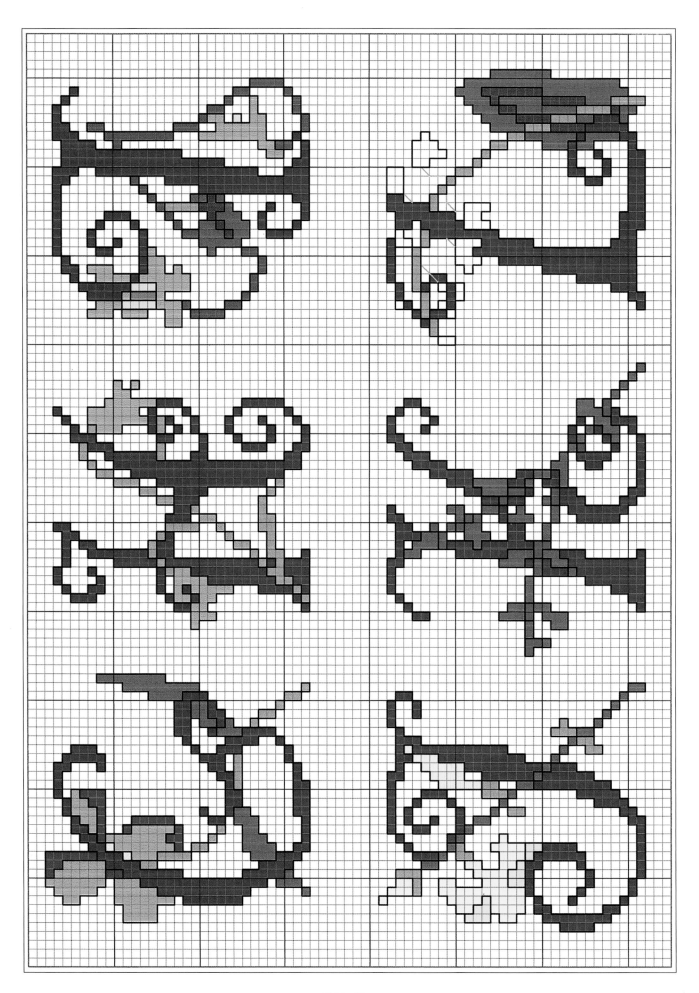

CHART 81

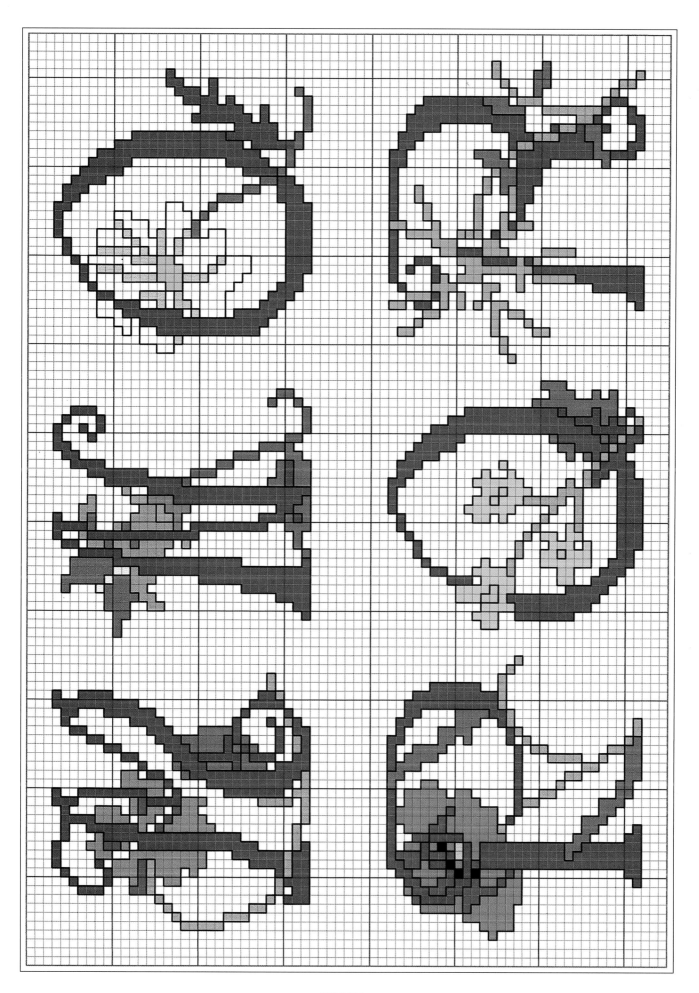

CHART 82

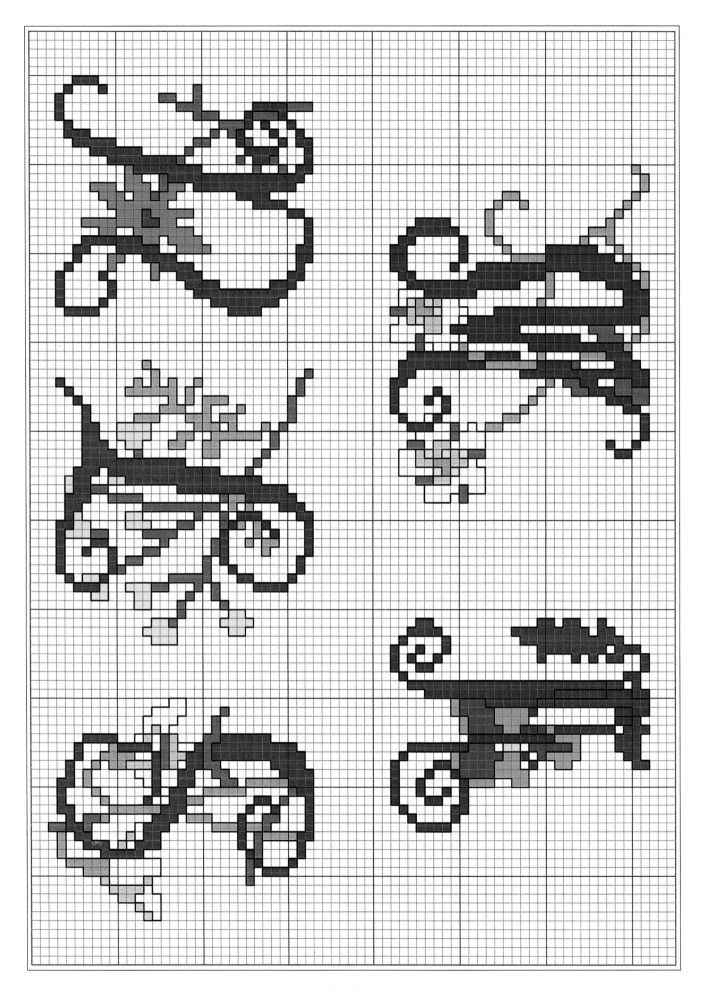

CHART 83

CHART 84

CHART 85

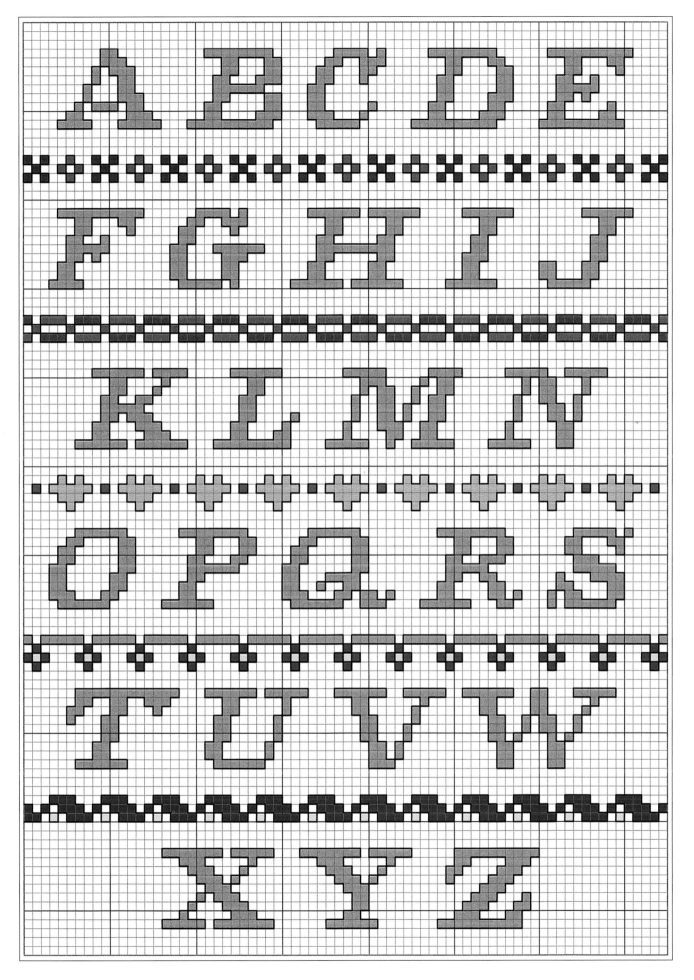

CHART 86

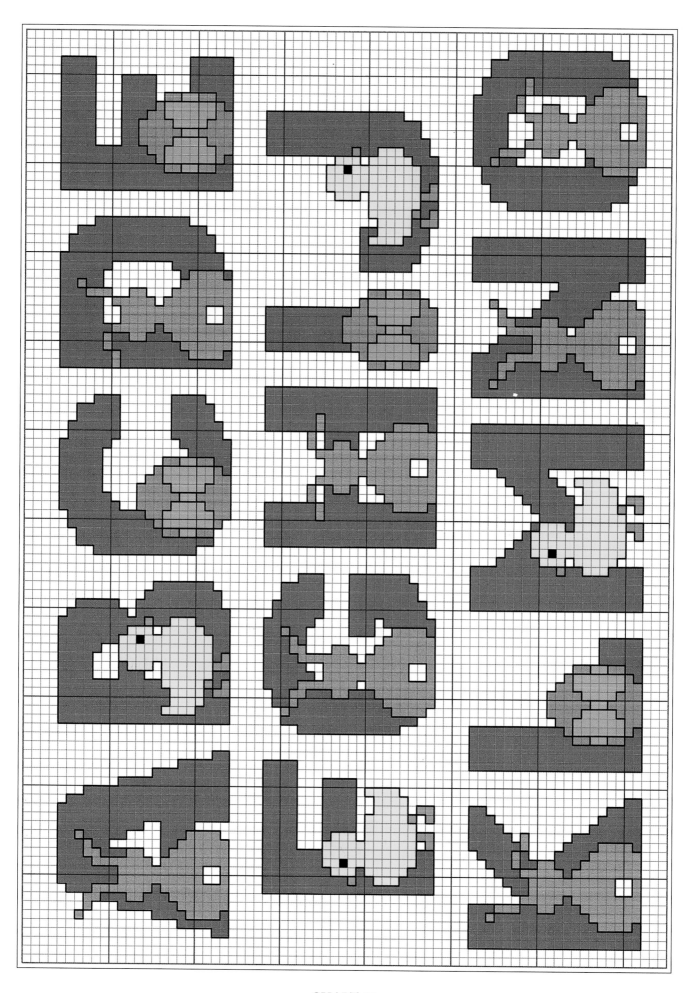

CHART 87

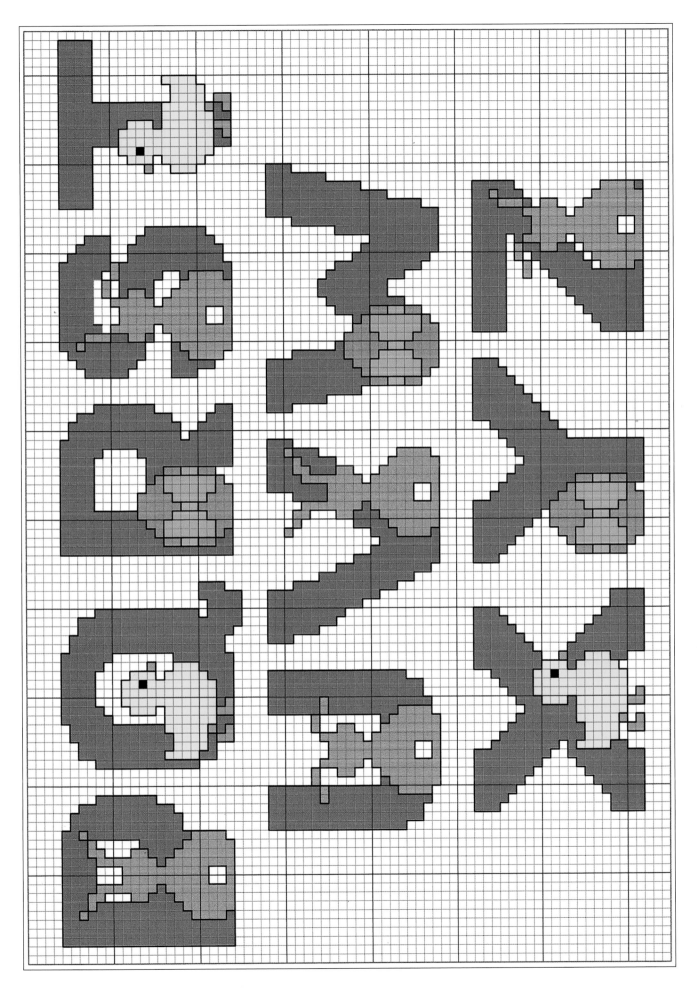

CHART 88

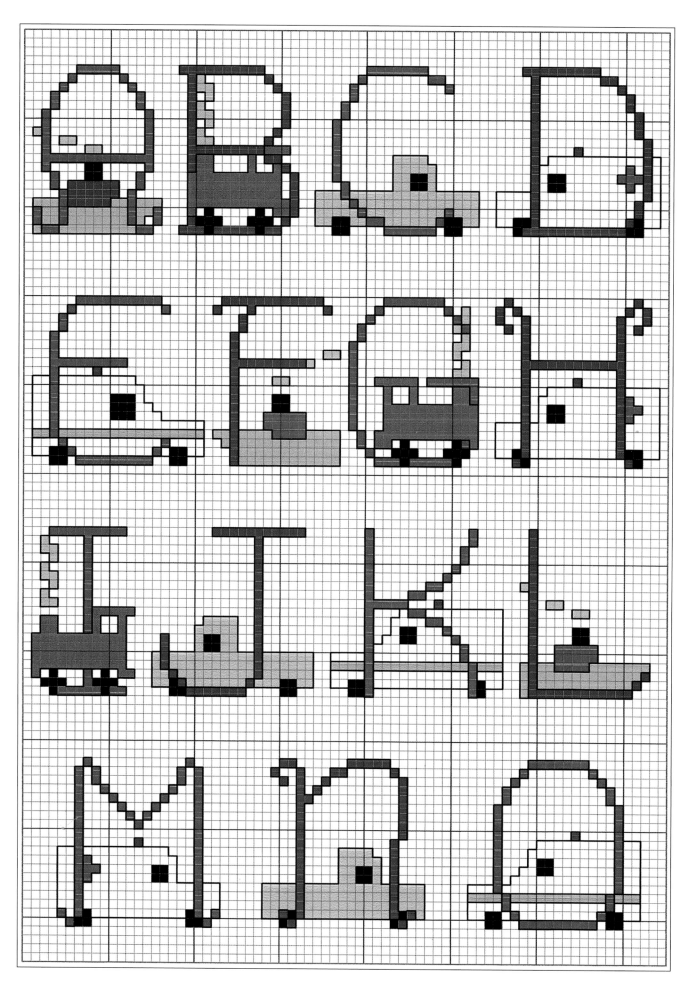

CHART 89

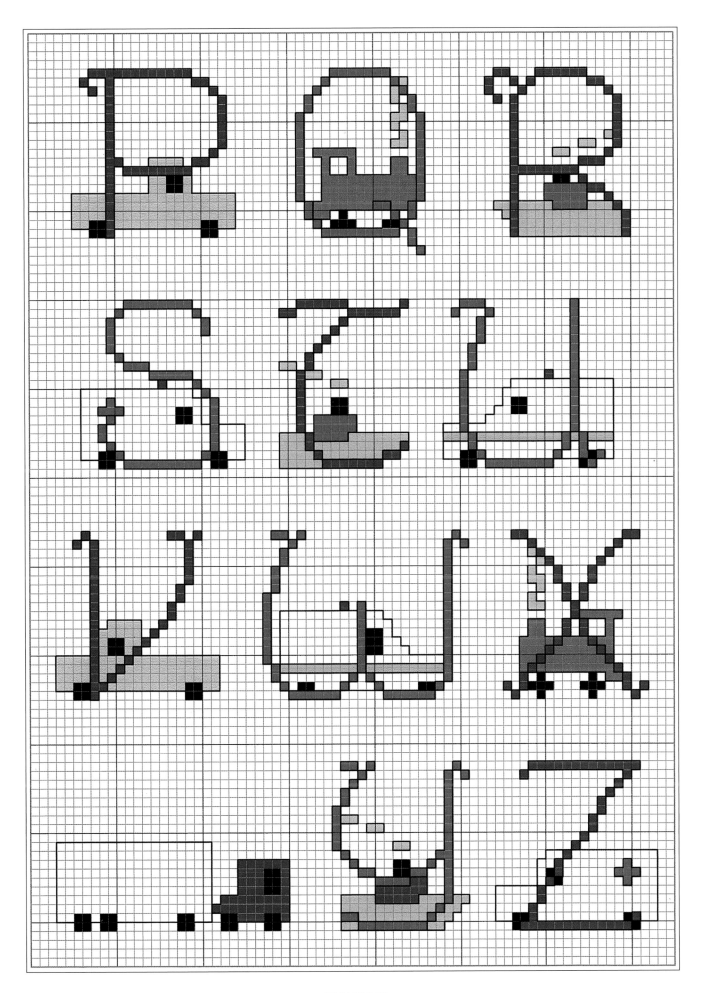

CHART 90

CHART 91

CHART 92

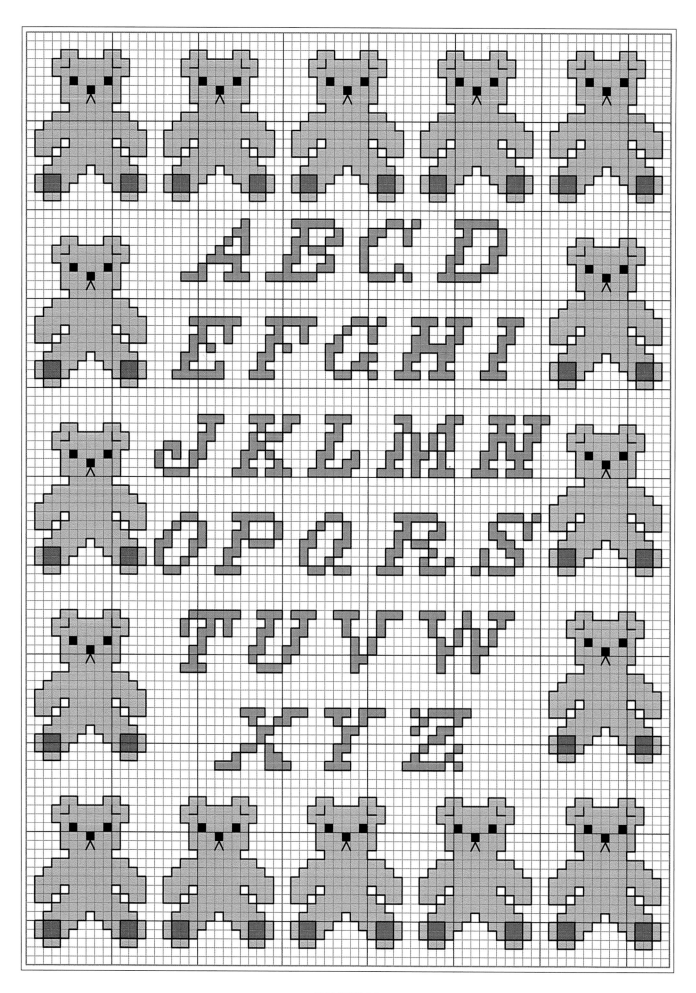

CHART 93

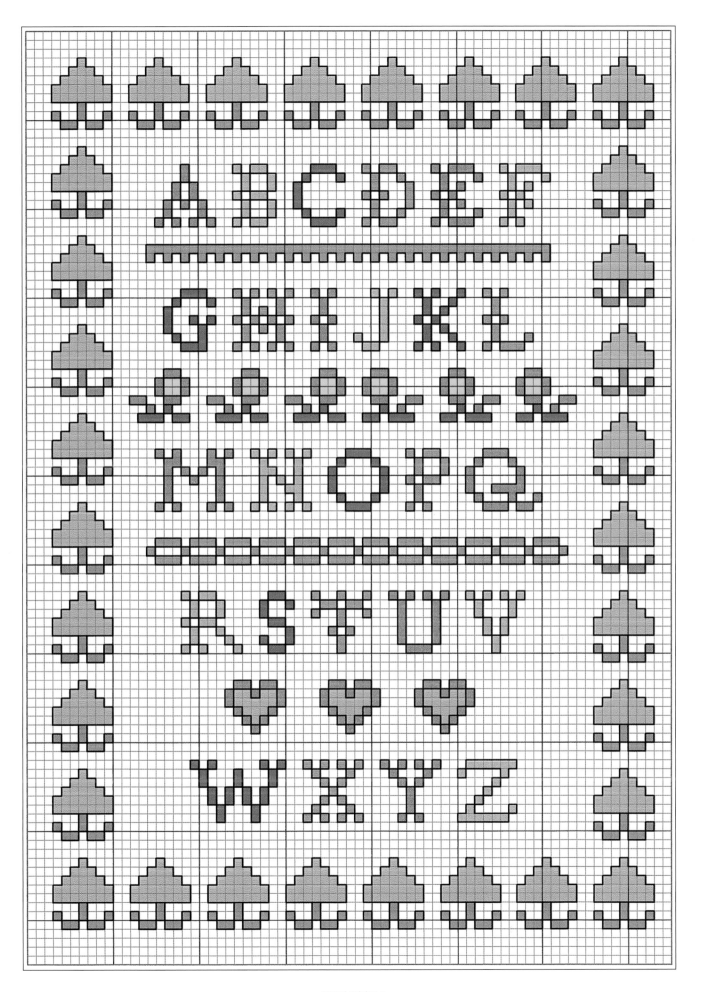

CHART 94

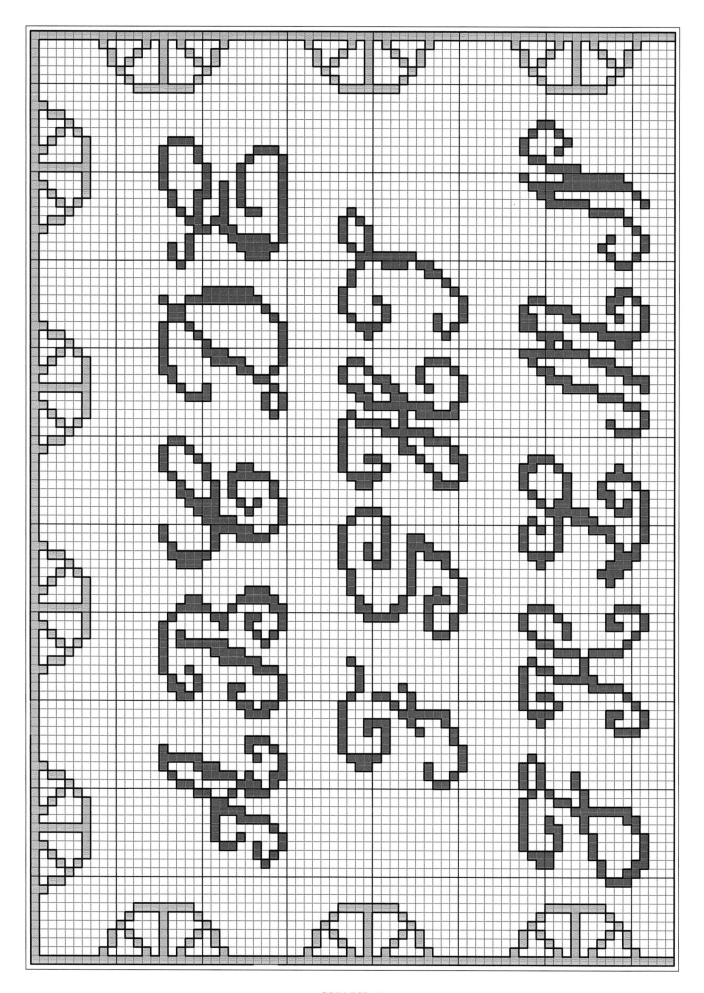

CHART 95

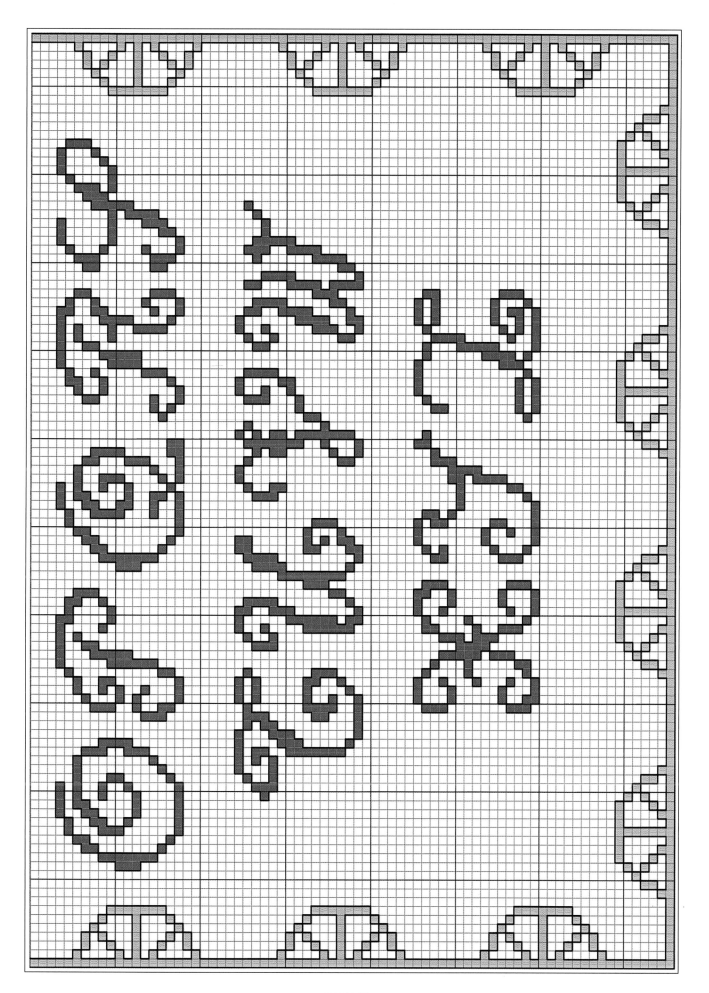

CHART 96

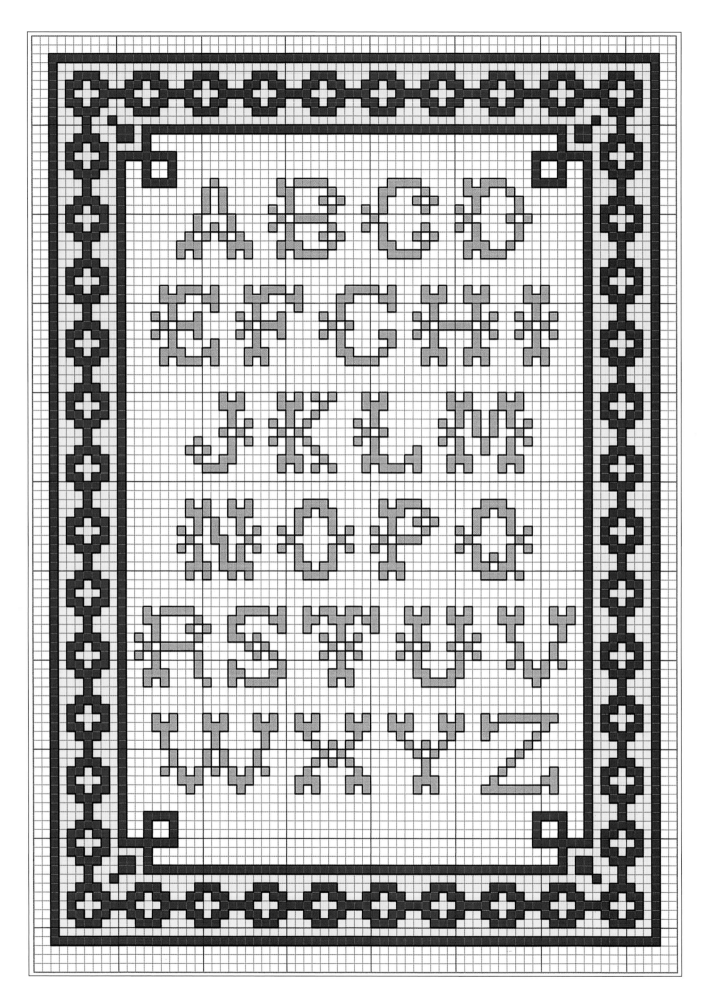

CHART 97

CHART 98

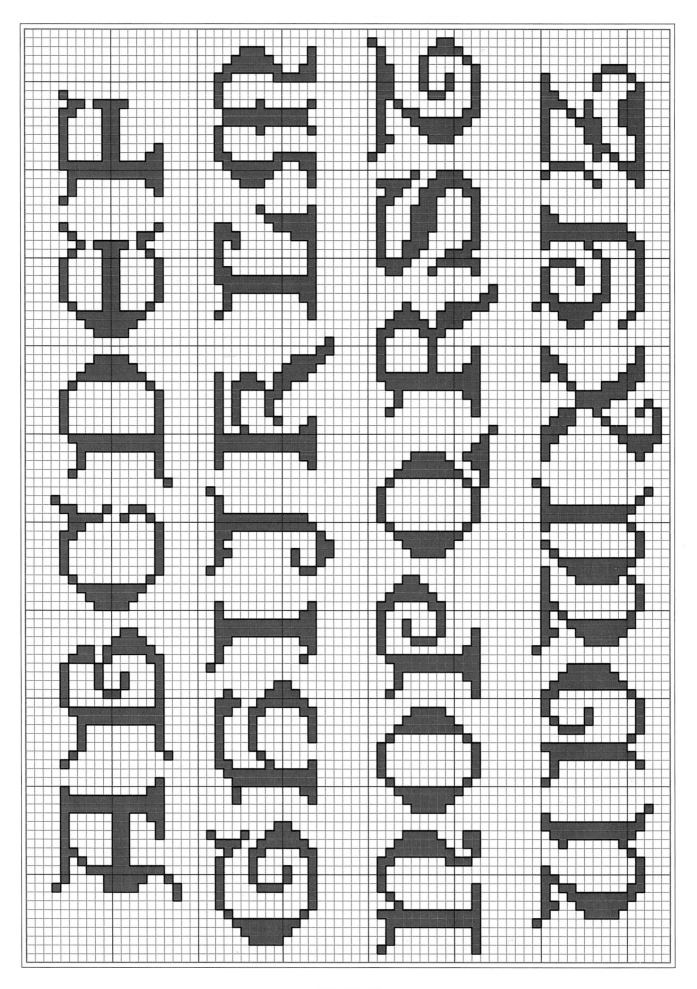

CHART 99

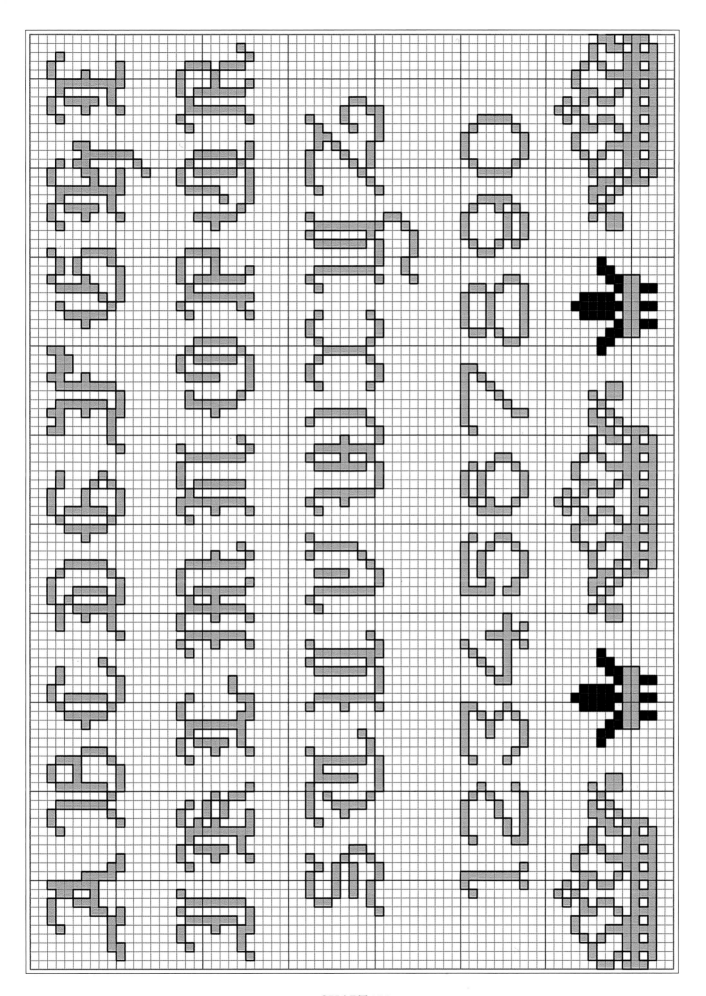

CHART 100

CHART 101

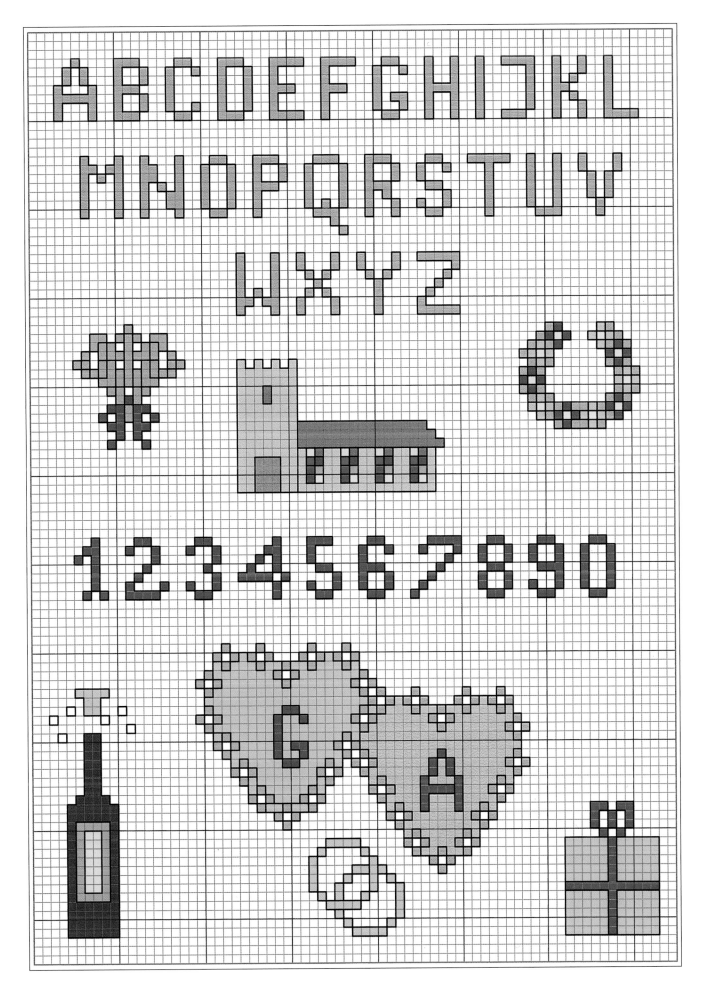

CHART 102

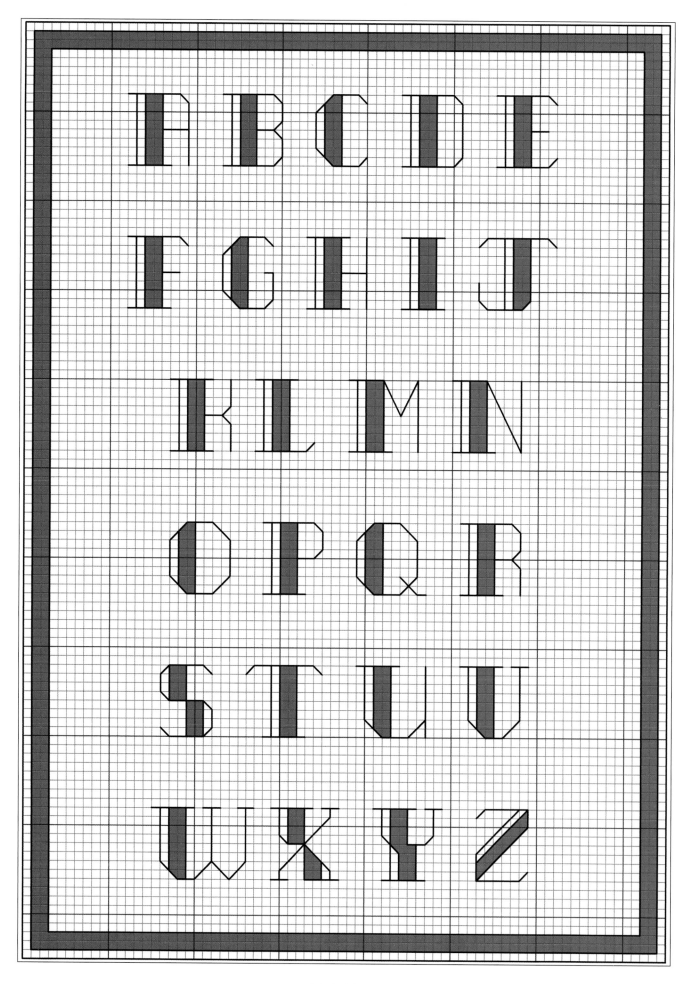

CHART 103

CHART 104

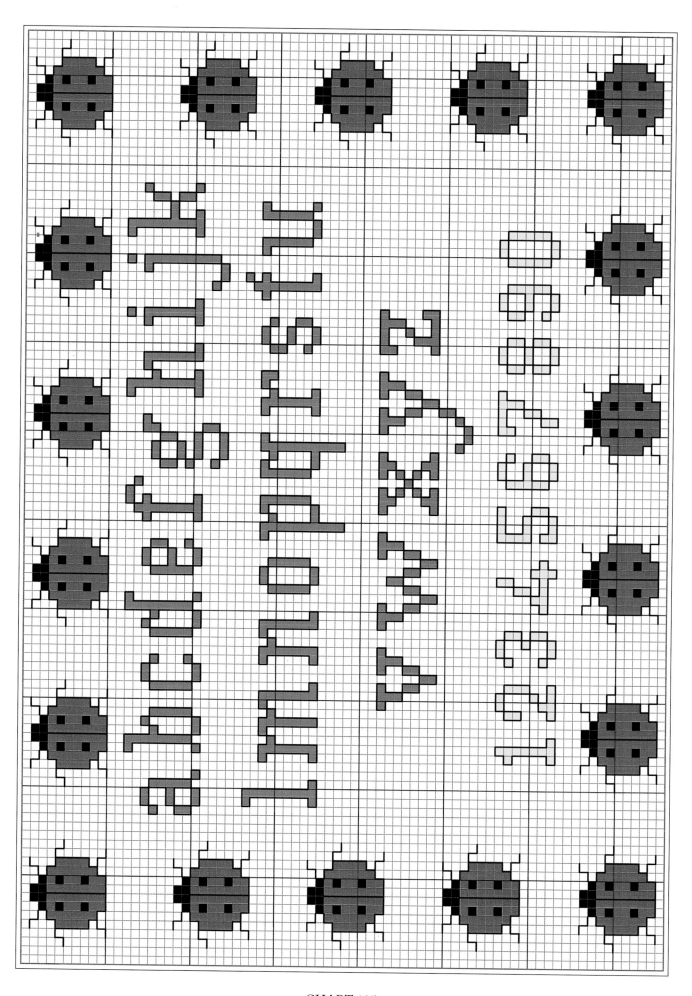

abcdefghijk
lmnopqrstu
vwxyz
abcdefghij
klmnopqrst

CHART 105

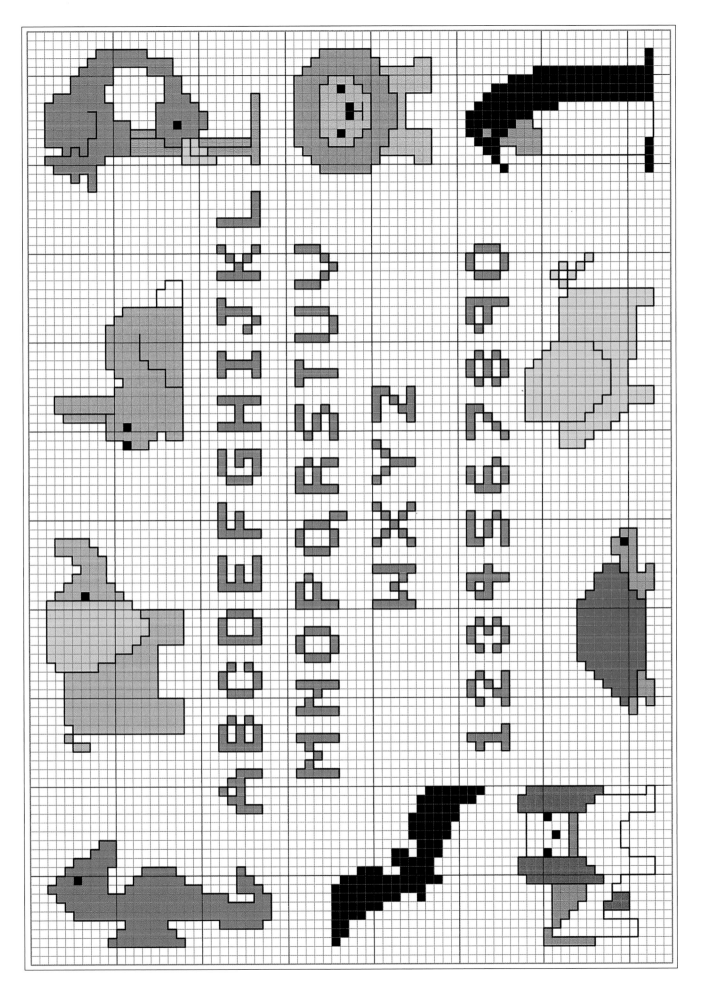

CHART 106

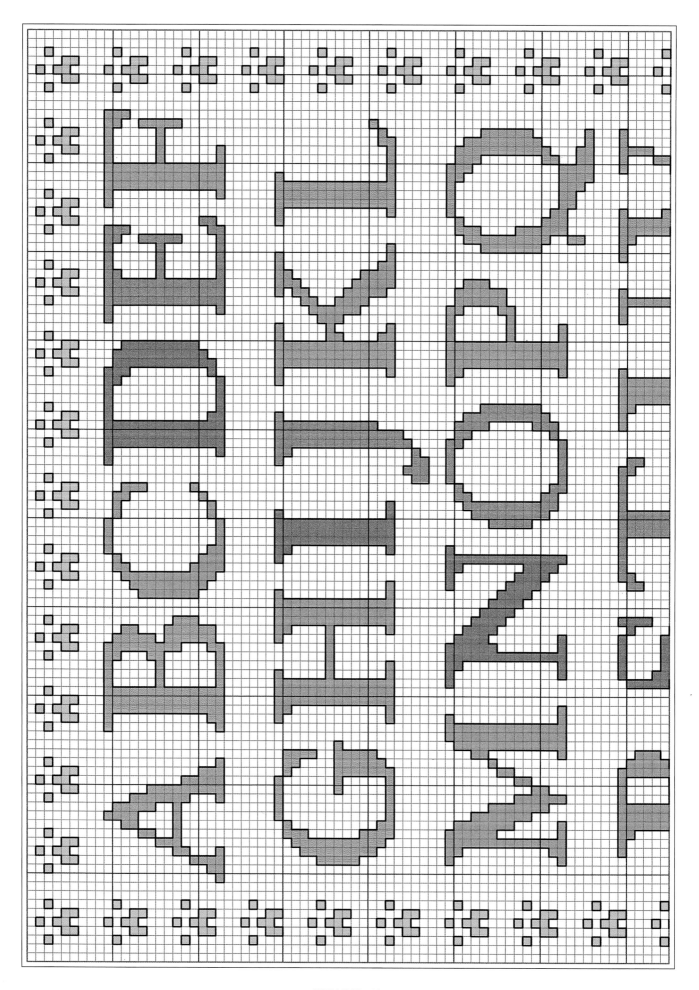

CHART 107

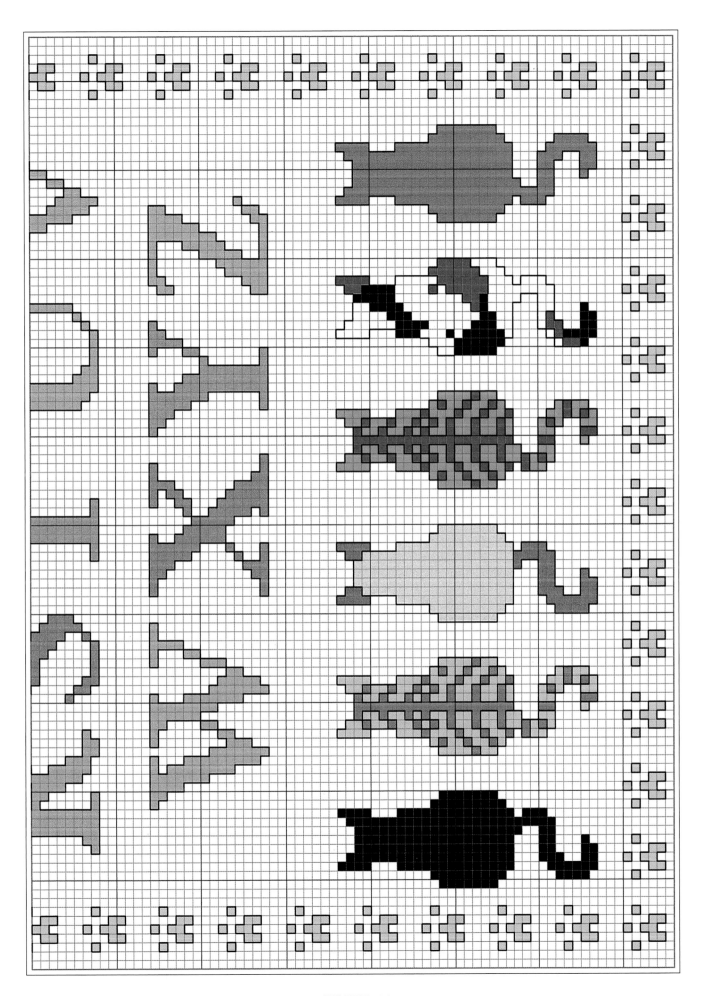

CHART 108

CHART 109

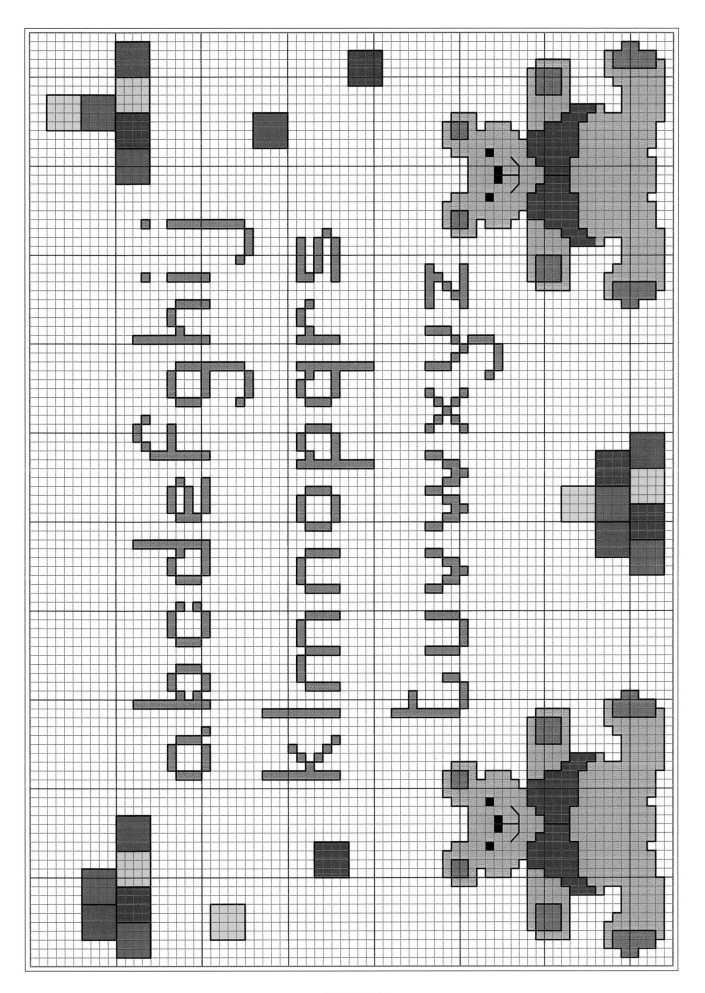

CHART 110

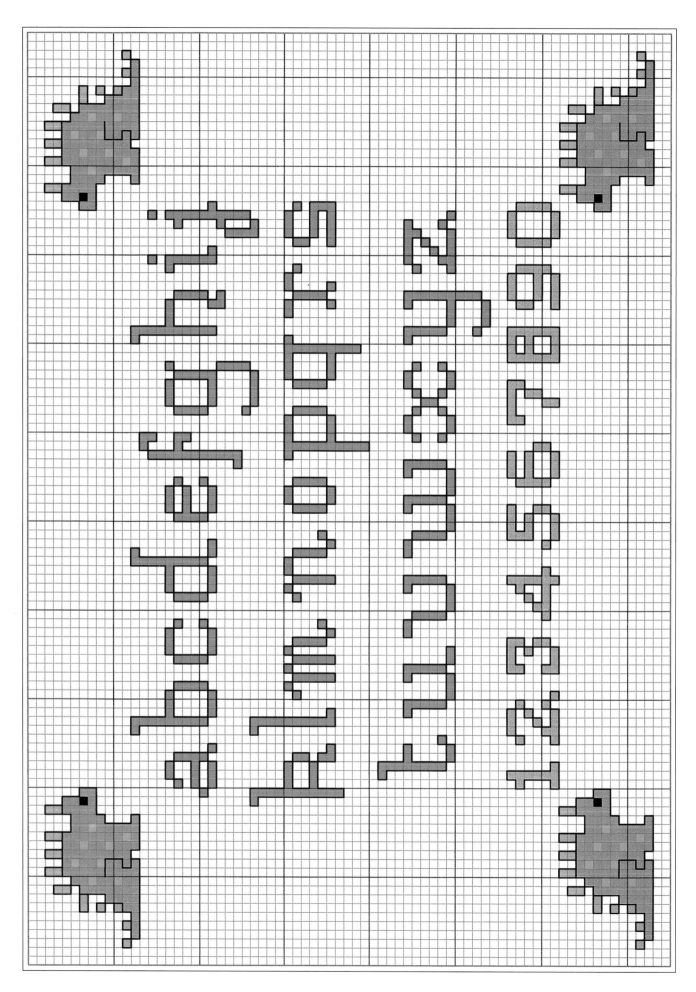

abcdefghij
klmnopqrs
tuvwxyz
0123456789

CHART 111

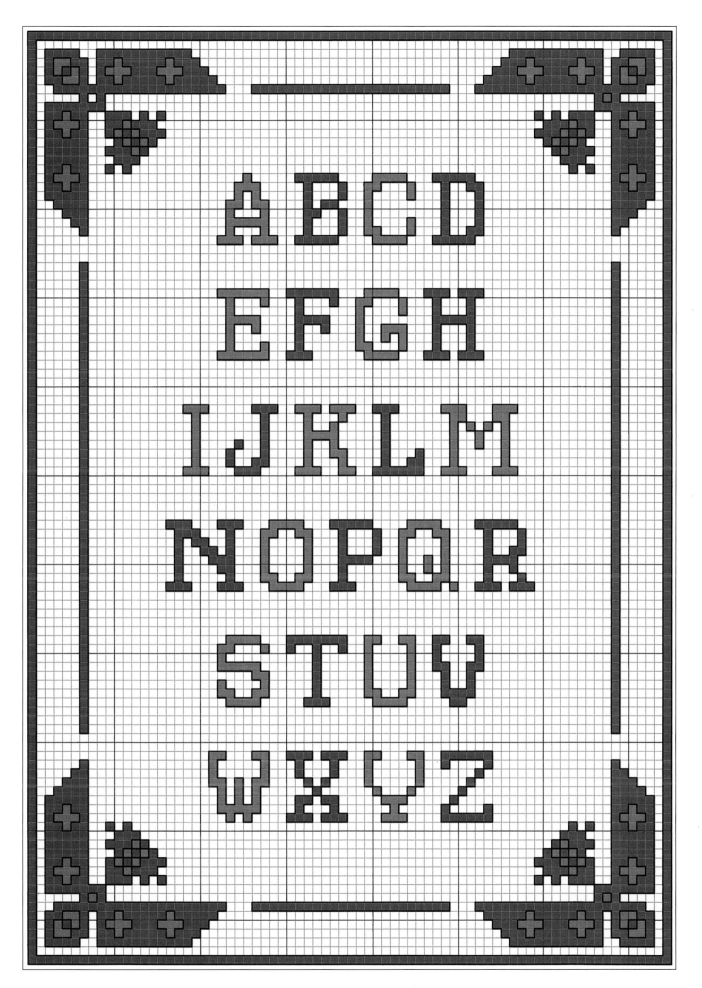

CHART 112

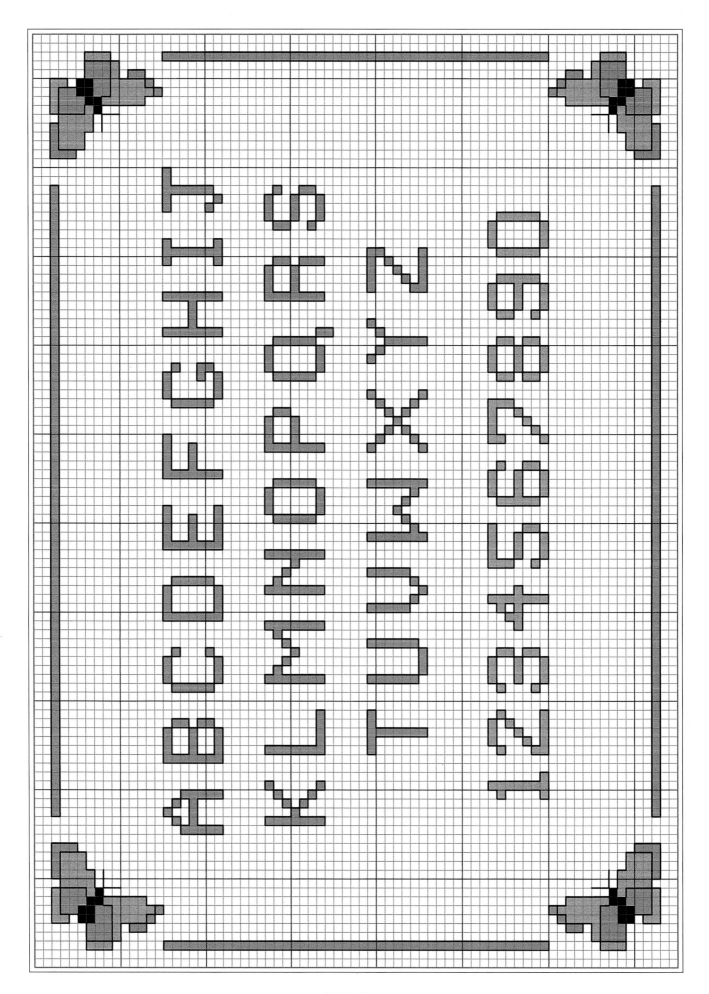

ABCDEFGHIJ
KLMNOPQRS
TUVWXYZ
1234567890

CHART 113

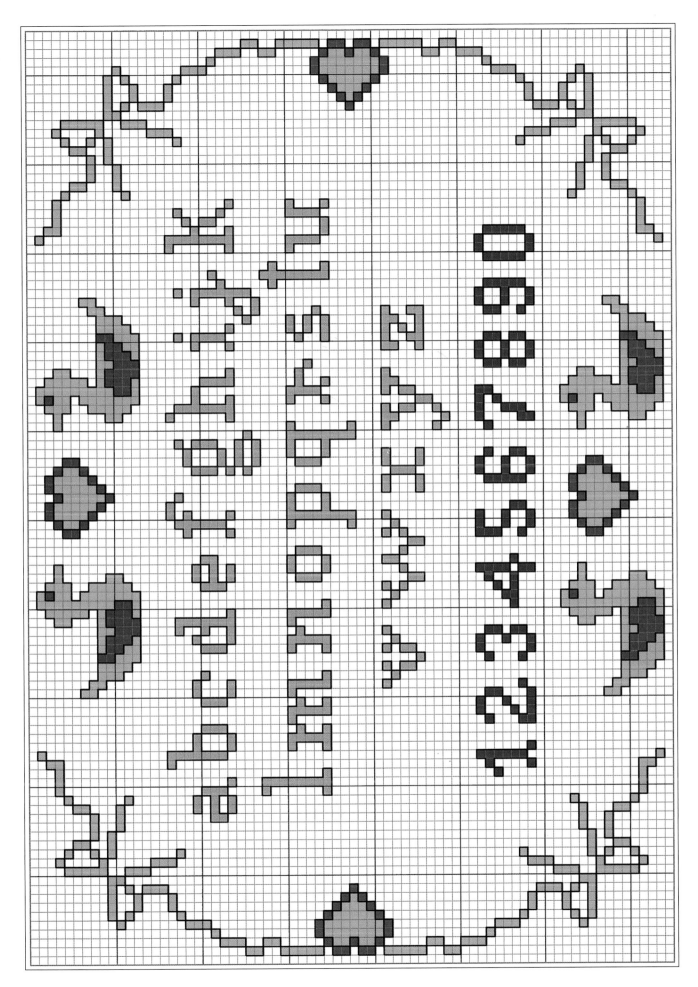

CHART 114

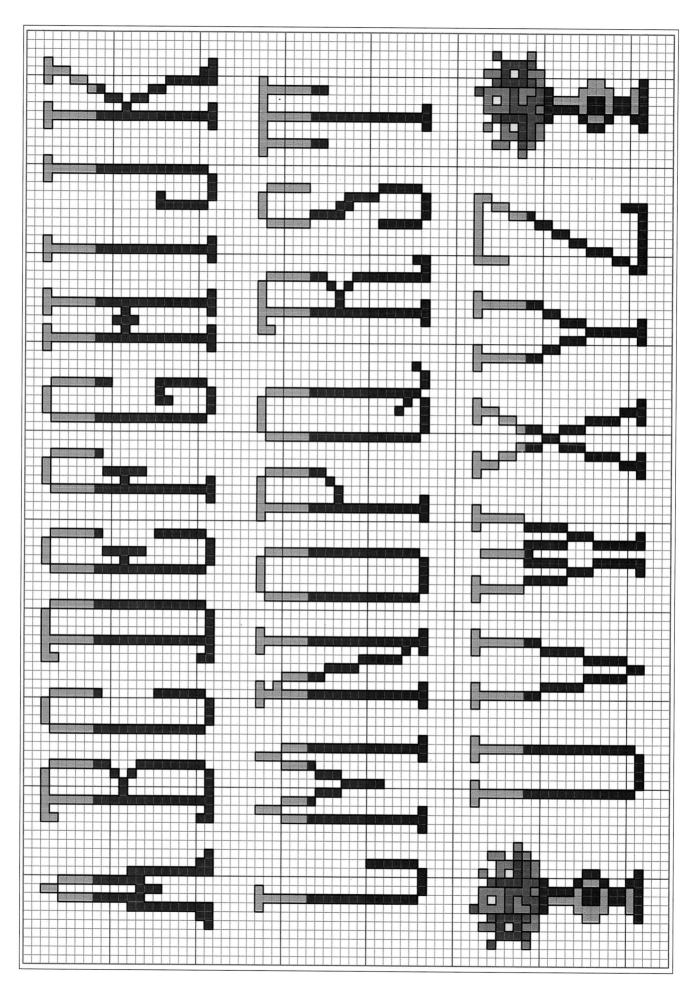

CHART 115

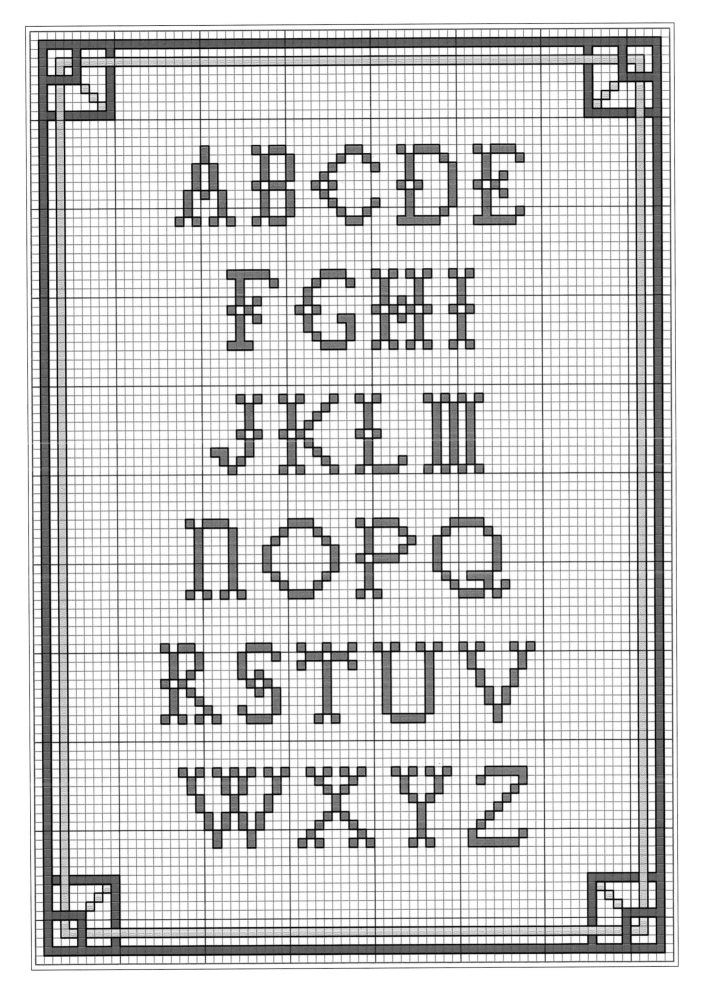

CHART 116

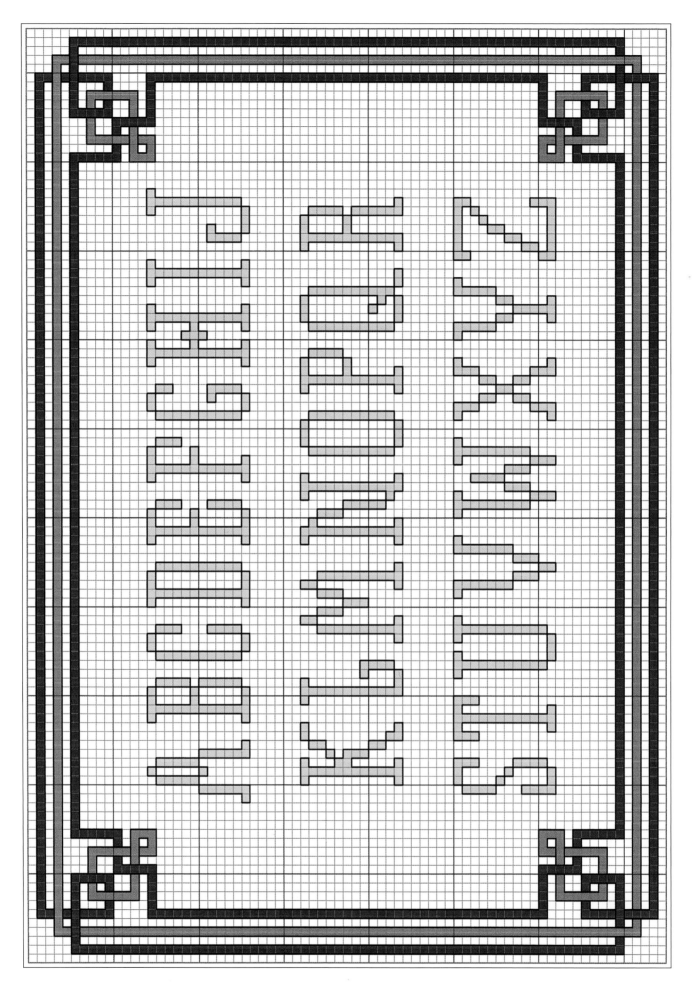

CHART 117

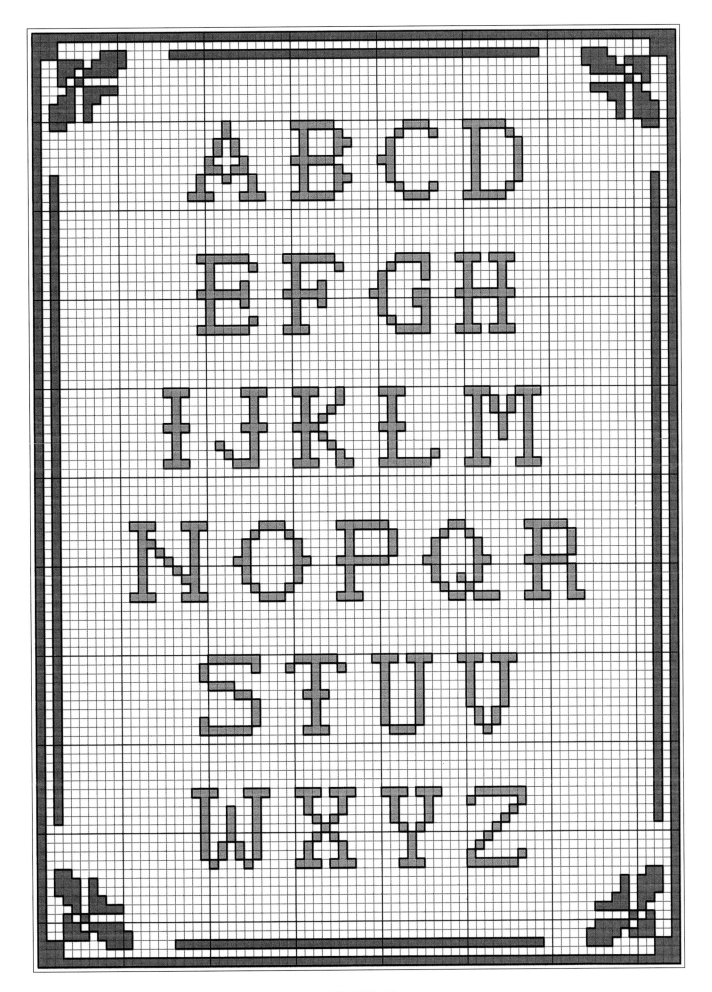

CHART 118

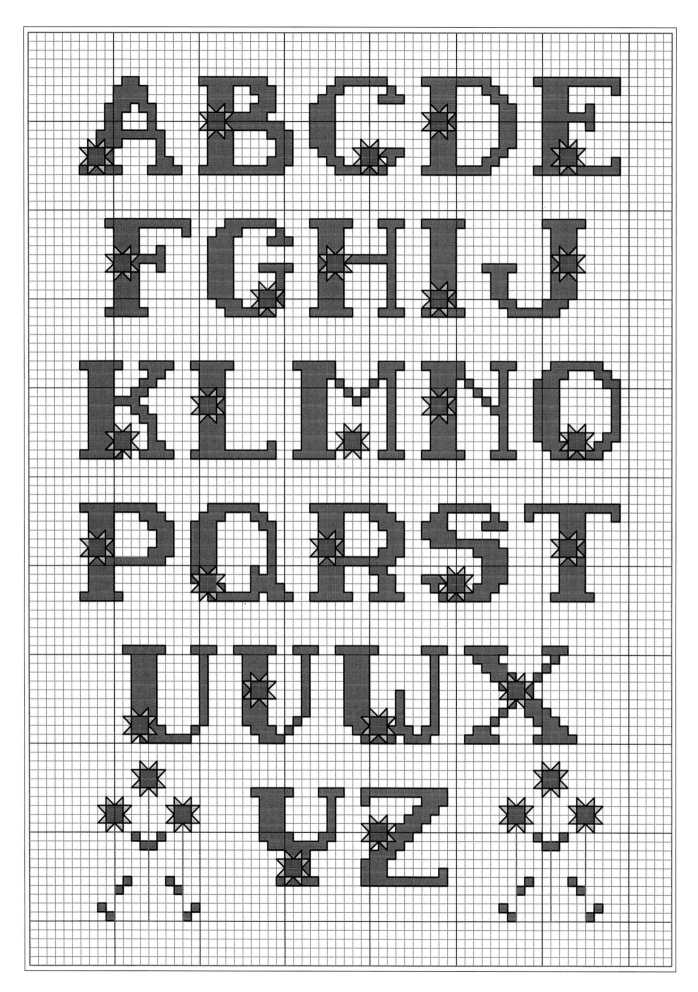

CHART 119

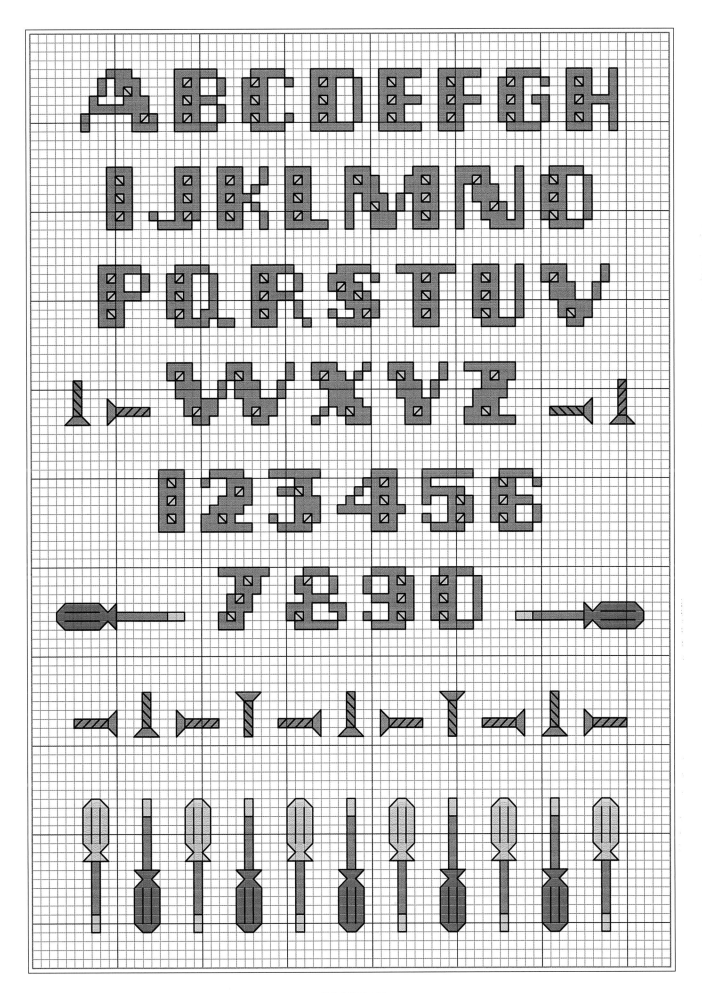

CHART 120

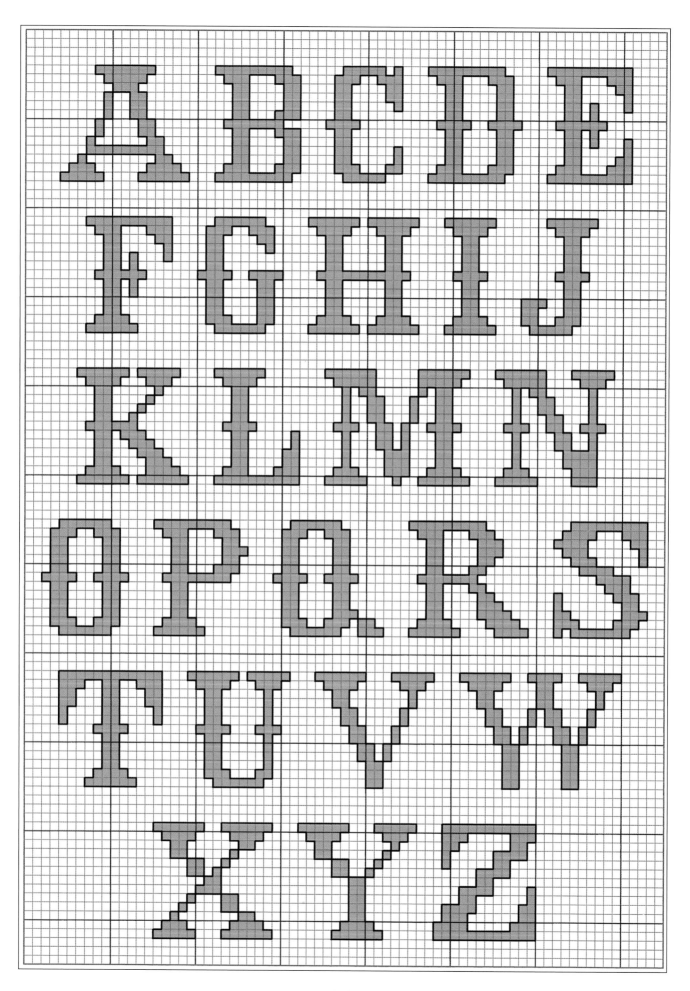

CHART 121

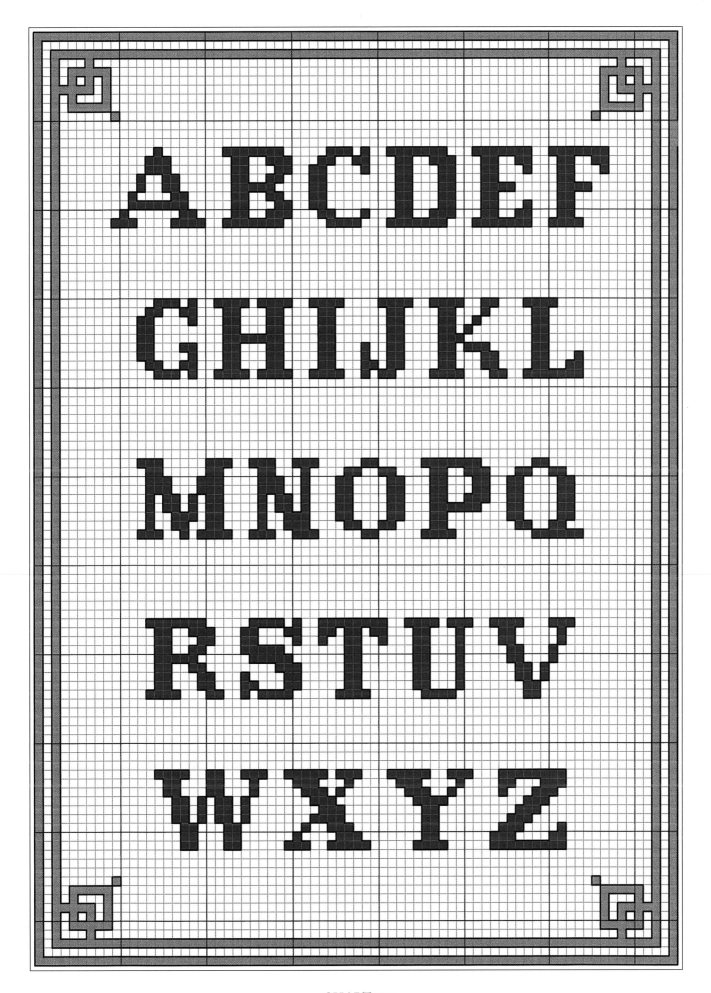

CHART 122

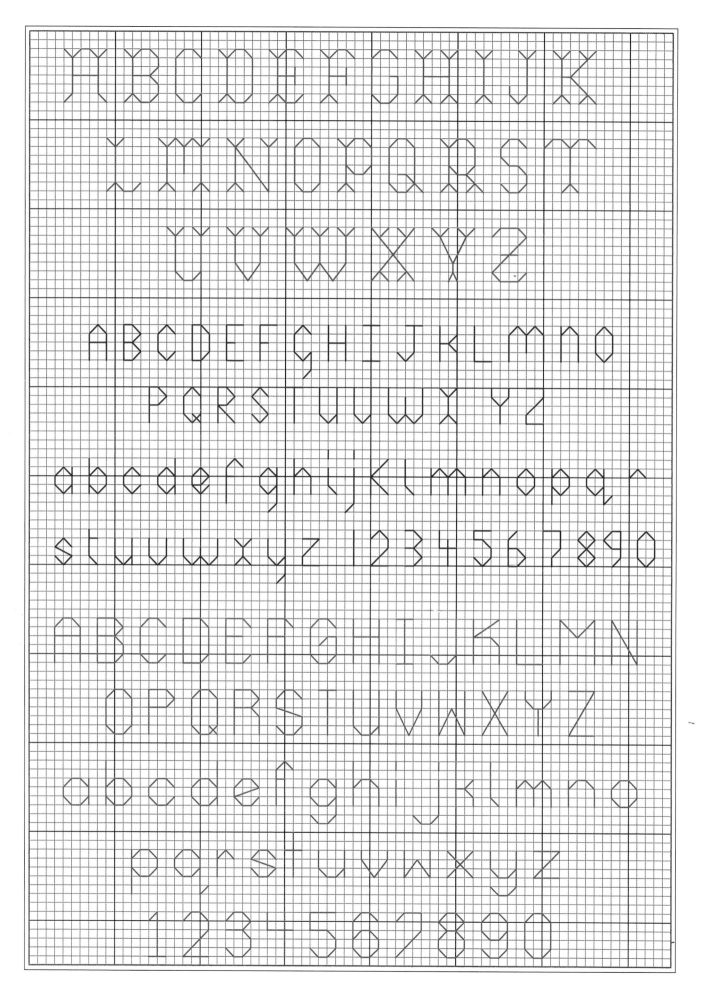

CHART 123

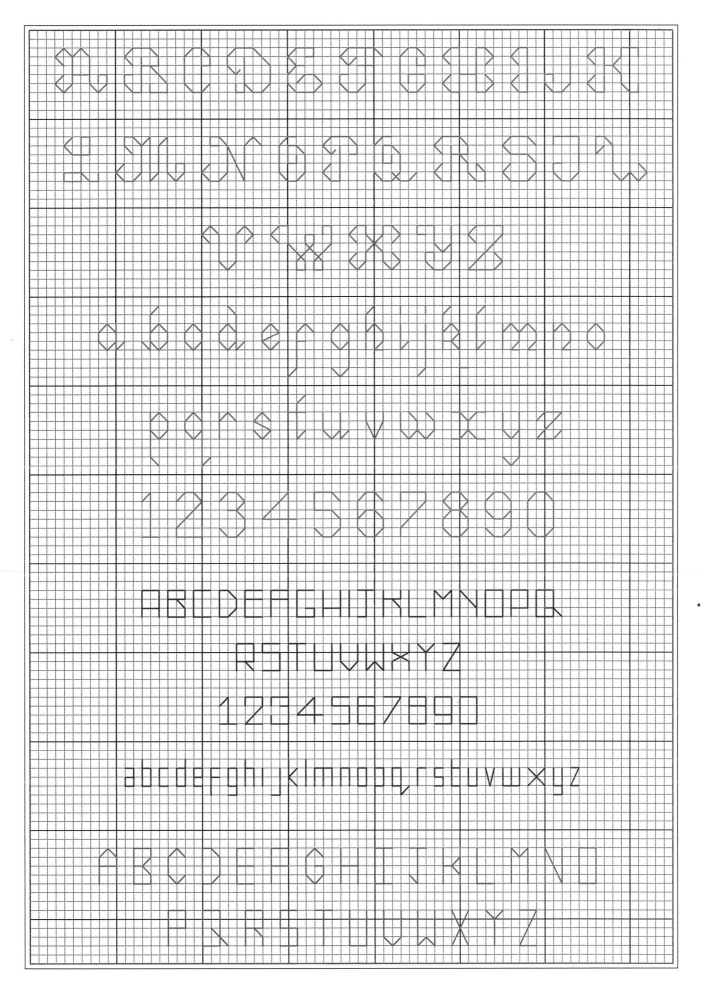

CHART 124

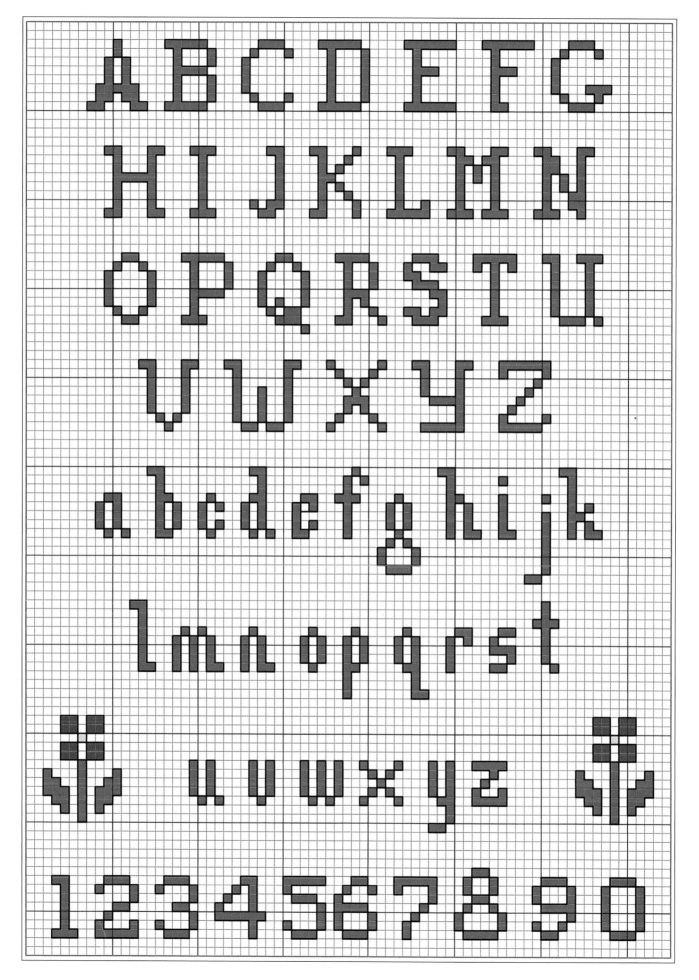

CHART 125

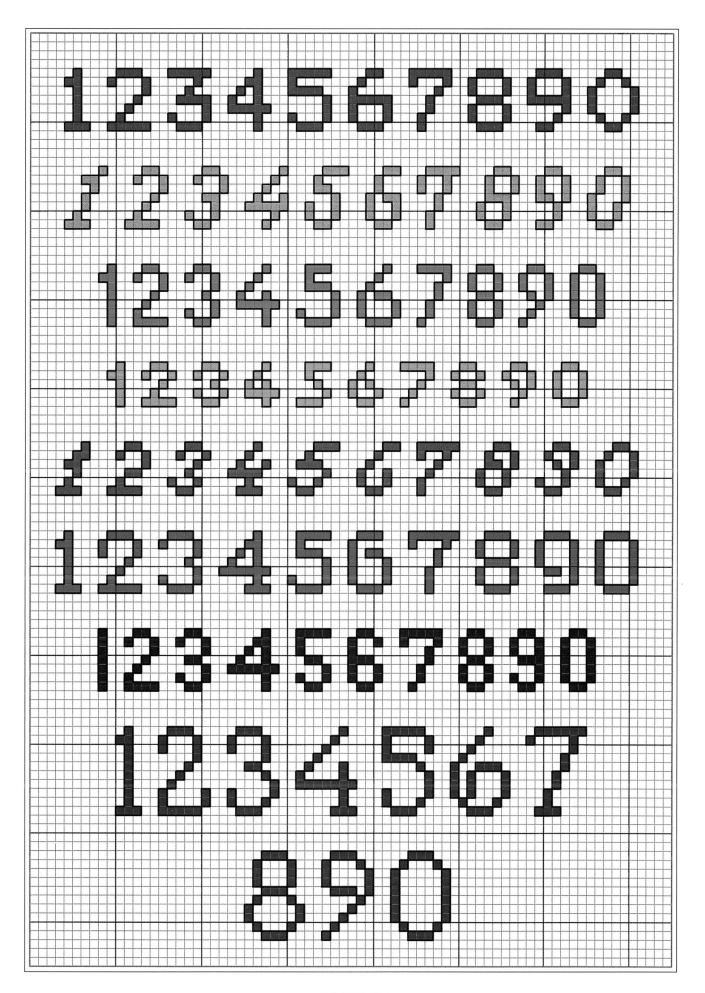

CHART 126

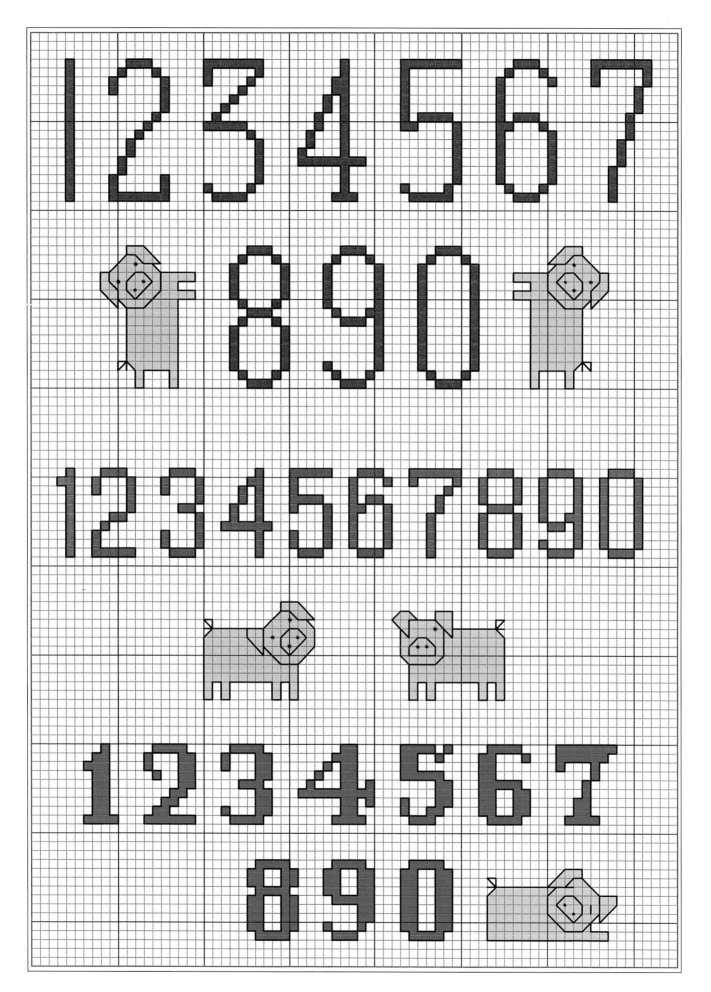

CHART 127

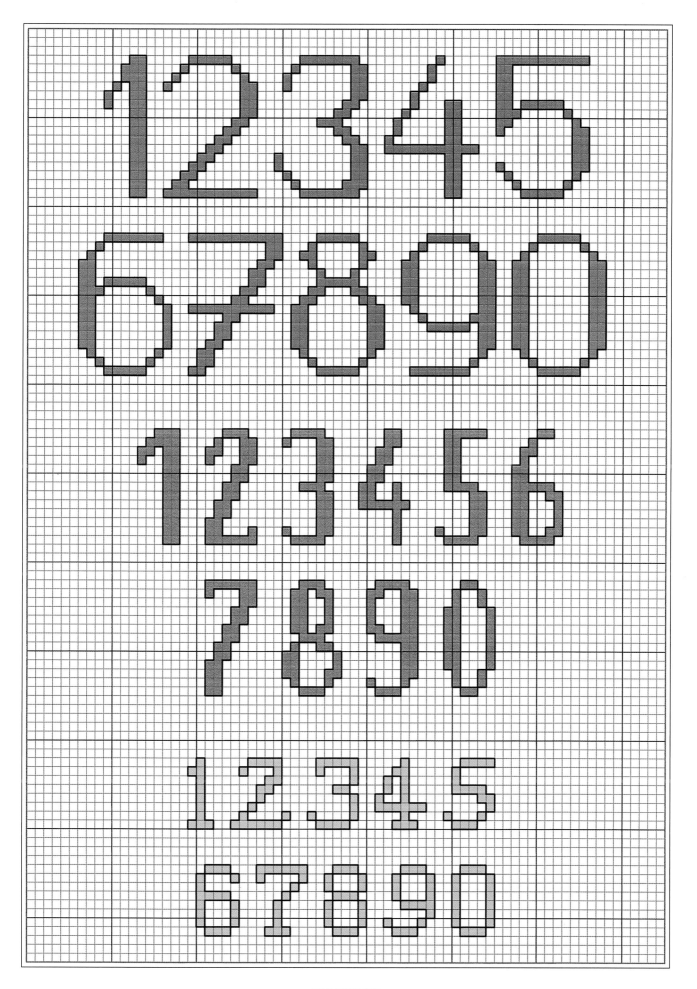

CHART 128

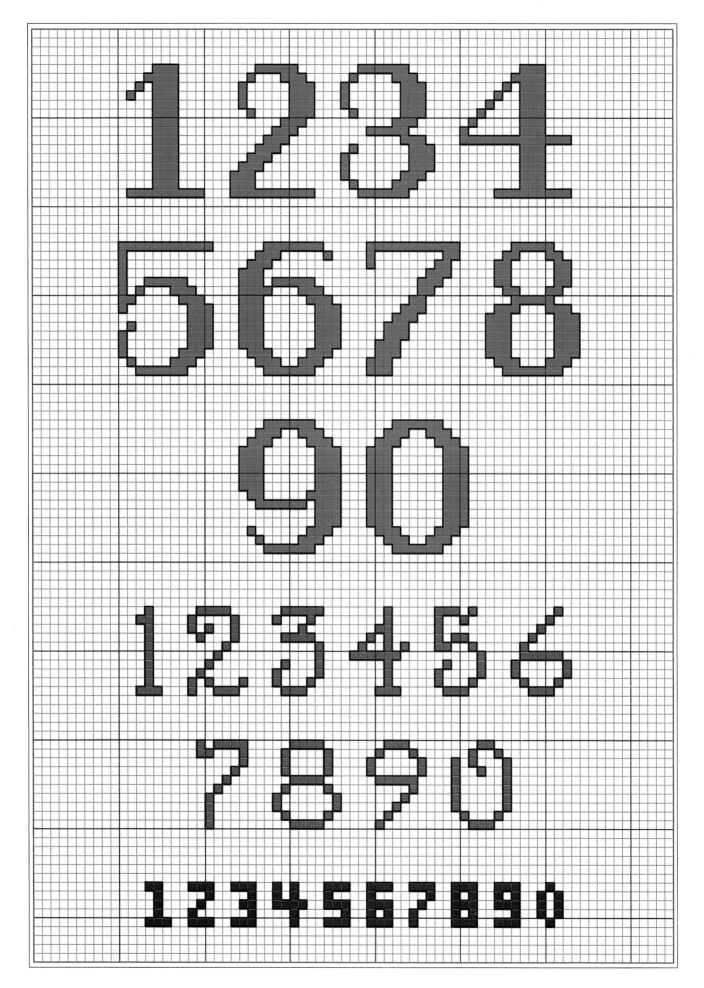

CHART 129